HALLOW

Fun Food & Crafts

pil

Publications International, Ltd.

Louis Weber, CEO
Publications International, Ltd.
7373 North Cicero Avenue
Lincolnwood, IL 60712

Pictured on the front cover *(clockwise from top left):* Halloween Chicken Pizza Masks *(page 34),* Sugar & Spice Jack-O'-Lantern Cookies *(page 24),* Hobnobbing Hobgoblins *(page 130)* and Spider Cupcakes *(page 59).*
Pictured on the back cover *(clockwise from top left):* Hot Cocoa with Floating Eyeballs *(page 80),* Tomb Many Days to Count *(page 101)* and Creepy Hands *(page 22).*

ISBN-13: 978-1-60553-703-0
ISBN-10: 1-60553-703-9

Library of Congress Control Number: 2009943761

Manufactured in China.

8 7 6 5 4 3 2 1

Microwave Cooking: Microwave ovens vary in wattage. Use the cooking times guidelines and check for doneness before adding more time.

Preparation/Cooking Times: Preparation times are based on the approximate amount of time required to assemble the recipe before cooking, baking, chilling or serving. These times include preparation steps such as measuring, chopping and mixing. The fact that some preparations and cooking can be done simultaneously is taken into account. Preparation of optional ingredients and serving suggestions is not included.

Patterns: PIL grants the holder of this book the right to photocopy patterns in this book, solely for the individual's noncommercial use, in their personal craft project(s) and will hold copy centers harmless when making fewer than three copies of each pattern.

pil

Publications International, Ltd.

Table of Contents

Mac & Cheese Jack-O'-Lanterns

8 (4-inch) individual aluminum pie tins or individual ramekins
8 ounces uncooked elbow macaroni
3 tablespoons butter
3 tablespoons flour
$2^1/_2$ cups milk
$^1/_2$ teaspoon onion powder
$^1/_2$ teaspoon salt
$^1/_8$ teaspoon black pepper (optional)
2 cups (8 ounces) shredded Cheddar cheese, divided
  Zucchini slices, olives, celery slices, carrot slices, radish slices, peas, green onions and/or broccoli

1. Preheat oven to 375°F. Spray pie tins or ramekins with nonstick cooking spray; place on baking sheet. Prepare macaroni according to package direction drain.

2. Melt butter in medium saucepan over medium heat. Stir in flour and cook 1 minute. Slowly whisk in milk. Cook and stir 5 to 7 minutes or until sauce thickens. Stir in onion powder, salt and pepper, if desired. Remove saucepan fro heat. Stir in $1^1/_2$ cups cheese; stir until melted.

3. Pour sauce over cooked macaroni and stir until well coated. Divide mixture among pie tins or ramekins and sprinkle remaining cheese over top. Press light with spatula to flatten. Create faces using celery slices for eyebrows, zucchini triangles for eyes and nose, and green onion for stem. Decorate with additiona vegetables as desired.

4. Bake 10 minutes or until cheese is melted.   *Makes 8 servings*

Spider Web Pull-Apart Cake

1 package (9 ounces) cake mix, plus ingredients to prepare mix
   Red and yellow food coloring
1 container (16 ounces) lemon or vanilla frosting
1 tube (about 4 ounces) black decorative icing
2 black licorice sticks
1 small chocolate wafer cookie
2 miniature marshmallows

1. Prepare cupcakes according to package directions. Place 7 cupcakes in circle on serving platter. Reserve 5 cupcakes for later use.

2. Stir several drops of each food coloring into frosting until desired shade of orange is reached. Drop frosting by large spoonfuls onto each cupcake. Using small spatula, swirl frosting over all cupcakes so they stick together and top fairly smooth.

3. Starting at center and continuing to outside edges of cupcakes, pipe black icing in spiral pattern. Use toothpick or small knife to draw 6 lines from center to outer edges of cupcakes to create web pattern.

4. Cut licorice sticks into 4 equal pieces. Place on cake; top with cookie to make spider. Place small amount black icing on marshmallows; place on cookie for eyes. *Makes 7 servings*

Spaghetti and Eyeballs

1 pound ground beef
$^1/_2$ cup bread crumbs
$^1/_3$ cup milk
1 egg
2 tablespoons finely chopped onion
$^1/_2$ teaspoon garlic salt
1 jar (16 ounces) large, pimiento-stuffed olives
8 ounces uncooked spaghetti
1 jar (16 ounces) pasta sauce, heated
Roasted red pepper slice (optional)

1. Preheat oven to 400°F. Spray baking sheet with cooking spray.

2. Combine ground beef, bread crumbs, milk, egg, onion and garlic salt in medium bowl; mix until blended. Shape mixture into 12 (2-inch) balls and place on prepared baking sheet. Press olive, pimiento end up, into each meatball to form eyeballs. Bake 15 minutes or until meatballs are browned and cooked through.

3. Meanwhile, prepare spaghetti according to package directions. Drain.

4. Toss hot spaghetti with pasta sauce; divide among plates. Top pasta with two eyeballs and pepper slice for tongue, if desired. *Makes 6 to 8 servinc*

Spaghetti and Eyeballs

Gushing Goo Rolls

12 soft corn tortillas
 2 tablespoons olive oil
 1 envelope (1$\frac{1}{4}$ ounces) taco seasoning mix
12 mozzarella-Cheddar swirled cheese sticks
    Nonstick cooking spray
    Cilantro sprigs or chopped cilantro (optional)

1. Preheat oven to 475°F. Line baking sheet with foil.

2. Place one tortilla on prepared baking sheet. Brush one side of tortilla with oil; sprinkle with 1 teaspoon taco seasoning. Top with one cheese stick and roll up tightly. Lay seam side down on prepared baking sheet. Spray top with cooking spray. Repeat with remaining tortillas, oil, seasoning and cheese.

3. Bake tortillas about 6 minutes or until cheese begins to melt.

4. Remove from oven. Let stand 3 minutes to allow oozing cheese to set slightly. Add cilantro sprigs or sprinkle with chopped cilantro. *Makes 12 rol*

TIP: Before assembling rolls, wrap tortillas with foil and warm briefly in the oven to make them more pliable.

Gushing Goo Rolls

Poison Apple Cupcakes

1 package (about 18 ounces) spice cake mix
1¹/₄ cups water
3 eggs
¹/₃ cup vegetable oil
1 apple, peeled and finely chopped
1 container (14 ounces) caramel apple dip or 1 container (14 ounces)
    glaze for strawberries
Assorted sugar sprinkles and decorative candies

1. Preheat oven to 350°F. Line 24 standard (2¹/₂-inch) muffin cups with paper baking cups.

2. Beat cake mix, water, eggs and oil in large bowl with electric mixer at medium speed 2 minutes. Stir in apple. Fill muffin cups about half full. Bake 20 minutes or until toothpick inserted into centers comes out clean. Remove to wire racks; cool completely.

3. Spread 1 tablespoon caramel apple dip onto each cupcake. Decorate as desired.

Makes 24 cupcakes

TIP: Look for tiered cupcake stands at craft and kitchen stores. They make ordinary cupcakes look extraordinary!

Poison Apple Cupcakes

Monster Mash Spread

1 package (8 ounces) cream cheese, softened
2 cups (8 ounces) shredded Monterey Jack cheese with jalapeño
 peppers
$^1/_2$ cup chopped green bell pepper
$^1/_4$ cup finely chopped green onions
 Green Onion Curls (recipe follows, optional)
 Assorted crackers

1. Line 8- or 9-inch round cake pan with foil. Spray with nonstick cooking spray; set aside.

2. Combine cream cheese, Monterey Jack, bell pepper and chopped green onions in medium bowl; mix well. Press mixture evenly into prepared pan. Cover; refrigerate 1 to 2 hours or overnight.

3. When ready to serve, invert pan onto large platter or serving tray; remove pan. Discard foil. Garnish with Green Onion Curls. Serve with crackers.

Makes 2 cups sprea

Green Onion Curls: Cut 3 or 4 green onions lengthwise into long, thin strips; place in bowl of ice water. Refrigerate until strips are curled, about 2 hours o overnight.

TIP: Substitute shredded Cheddar cheese for Monterey Jack cheese with jalapeño peppers. Drain 1 can (4 ounces) chopped green chiles and stir into cheese mixture before spreading into prepared pan.

Monster Mash Spread

Can of Worms

1 package (4-serving size) pistachio instant pudding, plus ingredients
    to prepare pudding
4 small clean cans with lids ajar*
16 gummy worms
    Neon blue or blue food coloring
2 cups whipped topping
4 tablespoons cookie or graham cracker crumbs (optional)

*If you prefer, you can use small Mason jars or clear plastic cups instead of cans.

1. Prepare pudding according to package directions.

2. Divide pudding among cans. Place 2 gummy worms in each can so they drape over sides.

3. Stir several drops of food coloring into whipped topping. Blend thoroughly

4. Spoon whipped topping into can. Sprinkle with cookie or graham cracker crumbs, if desired. Add additional worms as desired.　　※ *Makes 4 serving*

Cans of Worms

Meaty Bones

$^1/_2$ cup hickory smoked barbecue sauce
$^1/_4$ cup grape jelly
  2 tablespoons steak sauce
  1 teaspoon grated orange peel
    Nonstick cooking spray
12 chicken drumsticks, patted dry
    Salt and black pepper
12 pieces of gauze, 12 inches each

1. Preheat oven to 375°F.

2. Combine barbecue sauce, jelly, steak sauce and orange peel in a small microwavable bowl. Microwave on HIGH 1 minute or until jelly is melted. Sti to blend. Divide into two bowls.

3. Coat broiler rack and pan with cooking spray; arrange chicken on rack. Sprinkle lightly with salt and pepper. Broil 25 to 30 minutes or until cooked through (165°F), turning frequently. During last 5 minutes of broiling, baste chicken with half of sauce. Remove from oven.

4. Let stand 5 minutes to cool slightly. Wrap bottom portion of each drumstick with strip of gauze. Dip in remaining sauce.   *Makes 12 drumstic*

Meaty Bones

Shrunken Heads

4 small apples such as Gala, cored
Lemon juice
3 tablespoons packed brown sugar
2 tablespoons butter, melted
$^3/_4$ teaspoon ground cinnamon
$^1/_8$ teaspoon apple pie spice
Dash salt
Ice cream
Caramel ice cream topping
Chocolate chips
Halloween sprinkles (optional)

1. Preheat oven to 400°F. Spray 13×9-inch baking dish with nonstick cooking spray. Cut apples in half lengthwise; brush cut sides with lemon juice. Carve face into skin of each apple half.

2. Combine brown sugar, butter, cinnamon, apple pie spice and salt in small bowl; brush over all sides of apples, filling face cutouts. Place apples, cut side down, in baking dish. Pour remaining brown sugar mixture over apples in dish. Bake 18 to 20 minutes or until apples are tender.

3. For each serving, place scoop of ice cream in bowl and drizzle with caramel topping. Top with apple half. Add chocolate chips for eyes and top with sprinkles. *Makes 8 servings*

Stuffed Shrunken Heads: Preheat oven to 400°F. Brush apple insides with lemon juice. Carve scary face on one side of each apple. Combine $^1/_4$ cup brown sugar, 3 tablespoons melted butter, 1 teaspoon ground cinnamon, $^1/_8$ teaspoon apple pie spice and dash salt in small bowl; brush over outsides of apples. Place apples in baking dish. Add $^1/_4$ cup chopped walnuts, $^1/_4$ cup raisins and $^1/_4$ cup dried cranberries to brown sugar mixture; stuff into apples. Cover and bake 30 to 35 minutes or until apples are tender. Serve warm with whipped cream or ice cream. Makes 4 servings.

Shrunken Head

Creepy Hands

INGREDIENTS

8 cups popped popcorn
1 cup pumpkin seeds, cleaned and patted dry
$1/3$ cup butter or margarine, melted
1 tablespoon Worcestershire sauce
$1/2$ teaspoon garlic salt
$1/2$ teaspoon seasoned salt
Candy corn

SUPPLIES

6 clear industrial food-safe gloves
Orange and/or black ribbon
6 plastic spider rings

1. Preheat oven to 300°F. Place popcorn in single layer in 15×10-inch jelly-roll pan; sprinkle pumpkin seeds evenly over top.

2. Combine butter, Worcestershire sauce, garlic salt and seasoned salt in small bowl; mix well. Pour over popcorn; toss to coat.

3. Bake 30 minutes, stirring once. Cool completely in pan on wire rack.

4. Place candy corn in end of each glove finger for fingernail; pack glove tightly with popcorn mixture. Close glove tightly at wrist; tie with ribbon. Place ring on one finger of each hand. *Makes 6 serving*

Creepy Hands

Crusty Crawlers

1 cup *each* semisweet chocolate chips and peanut butter chips
3 cups crispy chow mein noodles
$3/4$ cup toffee bits
18 maraschino cherries, quartered and well drained

1. Place chocolate chips and peanut butter chips in large saucepan over low heat; stir until melted. Remove saucepan from heat; add noodles. Stir gently with rubber spatula until completely coated.

2. Spoon mixture into mounds on waxed paper. Sprinkle with toffee bits, pressing gently to adhere. Place two cherry pieces on each mound for eyes. Cool completely before serving. *Makes 36 crawler*

Sugar & Spice Jack-O'-Lantern Cookies

$2^1/3$ cups all-purpose flour
2 teaspoons ground cinnamon
$1^1/2$ teaspoons *each* baking powder and ground ginger
$1/2$ teaspoon salt
$1/4$ teaspoon nutmeg
$3/4$ cup ($1^1/2$ sticks) butter, softened
$1/2$ cup packed brown sugar
$1/2$ cup molasses
1 egg
Assorted Halloween decorations such as orange and black frostings and sprinkles

1. Combine flour, cinnamon, baking powder, ginger, salt and nutmeg in medium bowl. Beat butter and sugar in large bowl with electric mixer at medium speed until light and fluffy. Add molasses and egg; beat until well blended. Gradually beat in flour mixture just until combined.

2. Form dough into 2 balls; press into 2-inch-thick discs. Wrap in plastic wrap; refrigerate at least 1 hour or until firm. (Dough may be prepared up to 2 days before baking.) Let stand at room temperature to soften slightly befor rolling out.

3. Preheat oven to 350°F. Roll out dough on lightly floured surface to $1/4$-inc thickness. Cut out cookies with jack-o'-lantern cookie cutters or other shape as desired. Place cutouts on ungreased cookie sheets.

4. Bake 12 to 14 minutes or until centers of cookies are firm to the touch. L cookies stand 1 minute on cookie sheets; cool completely on wire racks. Fros and decorate as desired. *Makes 2½ dozen cook*

Crusty Crawlers

Feet of Meat

2¹/₂ pounds ground beef
¹/₂ cup bread crumbs or oatmeal
¹/₂ cup milk or water
1 egg
1 envelope (1 ounce) dry onion soup mix
1 clove garlic, minced
8 Brazil nuts or almonds
2 tablespoons barbecue sauce or ketchup

1. Preheat oven to 350°F. Combine ground beef, bread crumbs, milk, egg, onion soup mix and garlic in large bowl; stir until well blended. Reserve 1 cup meat mixture.

2. Divide remaining meat mixture in half; shape each half into 7×4-inch oval. Place ovals on rimmed baking sheet. Divide reserved 1 cup meat mixture into 8 balls; place 4 balls at end of each oval for toes. Press 1 nut into each toe for toenails. Brush meat loaves with barbecue sauce; bake 1¹/₂ hours or until cooked through (160°F). *Makes 8 to 10 serving*

 TIP: When shaping feet, form ankles that have been "cut off" and fill with dripping ketchup before serving for an especially gruesome effect!

Foot of Meat

Witches' Broomsticks

1 can (11 ounces) refrigerated French bread dough
1 egg yolk
1 teaspoon water
2 tablespoons grated Parmesan cheese
1 teaspoon dried oregano
2 (12-inch) pieces black string licorice

1. Preheat oven to 350°F. Lightly grease baking sheet.

2. Cut bread dough into 8 equal pieces; roll each piece into 10-inch length. Fold top third of dough down, leaving 3 inches at bottom. Twist doubled top two thirds to form broom handle. Cut bottom into 5 or 6 lengthwise strips to form bristles of broom. Place shaped dough pieces about 2 inches apart on prepared baking sheet.

3. Beat together egg yolk and water; brush evenly onto dough. Combine Parmesan cheese and oregano in small bowl; sprinkle evenly onto bottom portions of brooms.

4. Bake 15 to 20 minutes or until golden brown. Remove to wire rack; cool slightly.

5. Cut licorice evenly into 8 lengths; wrap around bottoms of brooms to "tie" bristles.

Makes 8 servings

Slimy Sliders

1 pork tenderloin (about 1 pound)
1 cup (8 ounces) barbecue sauce, divided
10 round (2½-inch diameter) dinner rolls, sliced and warmed
½ cup prepared guacamole
20 large pimiento-stuffed olives
20 decorative picks

1. Preheat oven to 450°F. Place tenderloin in small roasting pan; brush lightly with 1 to 2 tablespoons barbecue sauce. *To avoid cross-contamination, do not dip brush into remaining sauce.* Bake 30 minutes or until cooked through (160°F). Rest 10 minutes before slicing into thin slices.

2. Spoon about 1 teaspoon barbecue sauce onto roll bottoms (warm sauce first, if desired). Top sauce with 2 to 3 slices tenderloin. Spoon additional 1 teaspoon sauce over top. Spoon 1 to 2 teaspoons guacamole around edge of pork slices. Place tops on rolls.

3. Thread 1 olive onto each decorative pick. Push 2 picks into the top of each slider to form eyes. Serve warm. *Makes 10 sliders*

TIP: Substitute 1 (18-ounce) package shredded pork in barbecue sauce for the tenderloin and barbecue sauce. Heat according to package directions.

Slimy Slider

Friendly Ghost Puffs

1 cup water
$^1/_2$ cup (1 stick) butter, cut into pieces
1 cup all-purpose flour
$^1/_4$ teaspoon salt
4 eggs
1 quart orange sherbet
Powdered sugar
16 chocolate chips (optional)

1. Bring water and butter to a boil in medium saucepan over high heat, stirring until butter is melted. Reduce heat to low; stir in flour and salt until mixture forms a ball. Remove from heat. Add eggs, one at a time, beating after each addition until mixture is smooth.

2. Preheat oven to 400°F. Spoon about $^1/_3$ cup dough onto ungreased baking sheet. With wet knife, form into ghost shape 3 inches wide and 4 inches long. Repeat with remaining dough, spacing about 2 inches apart.

3. Bake 30 to 35 minutes or until puffed and golden. Remove to wire racks; cool completely.

4. Carefully cut each ghost in half horizontally; remove soft interior, leaving hollow shell.

5. Just before serving, fill each shell bottom with about $^1/_2$ cup orange sherbet. Cover with top of shell; sprinkle with powdered sugar. Position 2 chocolate chips on each ghost for eyes, if desired. *Makes 8 servings*

LOW EEN

Friendly Ghost Puffs

Halloween Chicken Pizza Masks

1 pound ground chicken
1/2 cup chopped onion
1 teaspoon salt
1 teaspoon dried oregano leaves
1/2 teaspoon ground black pepper
6 English muffins, split
1 1/2 cups prepared pizza sauce
1 large green or red bell pepper
1 cup (4 ounces) shredded Cheddar cheese
1 cup (4 ounces) shredded mozzarella cheese
1 can (2 1/4 ounces) sliced black olives, drained

Heat large skillet over medium-high heat until hot. Add chicken, onion, salt, oregano and black pepper. Cook and stir about 6 minutes or until chicken is no longer pink; set aside. Cover 15 1/2 × 10 1/2-inch baking pan with foil. Arrange muffins in single layer on prepared pan. Spread 2 tablespoons pizza sauce on each muffin half. Cover generously with chicken mixture, dividing evenly. Cut 12 slivers bell pepper into "smiling" mouth shapes; set aside. Chop remaining bell pepper; sprinkle over mini-pizzas. Combine Cheddar and mozzarella cheeses in small bowl; sprinkle generously over mini-pizzas. Bake at 450°F 12 minutes or until cheese is light brown. Make face on each pizza by using 2 olive slices for "eyes" and 1 pepper shape for "mouth."

Makes 12 mini pizz

Favorite recipe from *National Chicken Council*

Halloween Chicken Pizza Masks

Mini Pickle Sea Monster Burgers

4 large hamburger buns
2 whole dill pickles
1 pound ground beef
2 tablespoons steak sauce
  Salt and black pepper
3 American cheese slices, cut into 4 squares each
  Ketchup

1. Preheat broiler. Spray broiler rack and pan with nonstick cooking spray; set aside.

2. Cut 3 circles out of each bun half with 2-inch biscuit cutter; set aside. (Discard scraps or use to make bread crumbs for another use.)

3. Slice pickles lengthwise into thin slices. Using 12 largest slices, cut 4 to 5 slits on one end of each slice, about $1/2$ inch deep; fan slightly to resemble fish tails. Set aside. Save remaining slices for another use.

4. Combine ground beef and steak sauce in medium bowl; mix just until blended. Shape meat into 12 ($2^{1}/_{2} \times {}^{1}/_{4}$-inch) patties. Place on broiler rack. Sprinkle with salt and pepper. Broil 4 inches from heat 2 minutes. Turn patties and broil 2 minutes or until no longer pink in center. Remove from heat; top with cheese squares.

5. Arrange bun bottoms on serving platter; top with ketchup and pickle slices, making sure slices stick out at both ends. Place cheeseburgers on top of pickles; top with bun tops. Place drop of ketchup on uncut end of pickle for eye.   *Makes 12 mini burger.*

Mini Pickle Sea Monster Burgers

Mummy Heads

4 cups mini marshmallows
1/4 cup (1/2 stick) unsalted butter
6 cups crisp rice cereal
1/4 teaspoon ground cinnamon
12 strips of gauze, each about 15 inches long (15 feet of gauze total)
24 dried cranberries

1. Place marshmallows and butter in large microwavable bowl. Microwave on HIGH 2 minutes. Stir 30 seconds or until completely melted. Immediately add cereal and cinnamon. Stir with rubber spatula until completely blended.

2. Spray clean hands with nonstick cooking spray and shape cereal mixture into 12 oval shapes. Re-spray hands while working with cereal mixture as needed.

3. Fold a strip of gauze in half lengthwise, making a 15 × 1 1/2-inch strip. Starting at one end, wrap around oval to cover it entirely, leaving a gap for eyes. When head is completely wrapped, unfold end of gauze slightly and press down. (Gauze will stick to surface.)

4. Place 2 dried cranberries in the gap for eyes and press to adhere. Repeat with remaining heads and cranberries.

5. Store in airtight container at room temperature.   *Makes 12 heads*

Mummy Heads

Eerie Ooze Turnovers

1 package (15 ounces) refrigerated pie dough
1 can (20 ounces) cherry pie filling
$1/4$ teaspoon almond extract
   Nonstick cooking spray
   Cinnamon sugar

1. Preheat oven to 375°F. Line baking sheets with foil; set aside.

2. Unroll pie dough; cut each into quarters. Combine pie filling and almond extract in medium bowl; stir until blended.

3. Spoon $1/4$ cup cherry mixture into center of each dough quarter. Fold edges over to form triangle; press together with tines of fork to seal tightly.

4. Place turnovers on prepared baking sheets. Spray turnovers with cooking spray; sprinkle with cinnamon sugar. Bake 15 to 25 minutes or until golden. Cool 5 minutes on baking sheets. Serve warm.   *Makes 8 turnovers*

Guacamole

2 large avocados, peeled and pitted
$1/4$ cup finely chopped tomato
2 tablespoons lime juice or lemon juice
2 tablespoons grated onion with juice
$1/2$ teaspoon salt
$1/4$ teaspoon hot pepper sauce
   Black pepper

1. Place avocados in medium bowl; mash coarsely with fork. Stir in tomato, lime juice, onion, salt and pepper sauce; mix well. Add black pepper to taste.

2. Spoon into serving container. Serve immediately or cover and refrigerate up to 2 hours. Garnish with additional chopped tomatoes, if desired.
Makes 2 cup

Eerie Ooze Turnovers

Freaky Fondue

4 (10-inch) spinach or tomato flour tortillas
1 cup canned cheese dip, Cheddar cheese sauce or salsa con queso
8 small carrots, peeled
8 almond slices
1 small jicama, peeled
1 cup cauliflower florets
1 tablespoon milk
1 tablespoon salsa

1. To make tortilla hands, heat oven to 325°F. Cut 1 tortilla in half. Cut each half into the shape of small hand; discard trimmed pieces. Place on baking sheet. Repeat with remaining tortillas. (To create curved hands, drape hands over a small bowl or custard cup before baking). Spray both sides of hands with nonstick cooking spray. Bake for 10 minutes or until lightly browned. Set aside to cool.

2. To make carrot fingers, place small amount cheese dip on narrow ends of carrots; top with almond slices for fingernails.

3. To make jicama bones, cut jicama into $1/4$-inch slices. Cut rectangle from each slice; trim ends of rectangles to create bones.

4. Arrange cauliflower brains, tortilla hands, carrot fingers and jicama bones on large platter. Stir milk into remaining cheese dip; microwave on HIGH 15 seconds or until warm. Spoon warm dip into small serving bowl. Swirl salsa on top. Place warm fondue dip in center of platter. Serve immediately.

Makes 8 to 10 servings

Freaky Fondue

Incredible Edible Fortune Teller's Ball

1 package (6 ounces) orange gelatin
1 package (3 ounces) lemon gelatin
3 cups boiling water
1 large red apple
2 tablespoons lemon or orange juice
$^1/_4$ cup blueberries
    Mandarin oranges and blueberries (optional)

1. Combine orange and lemon gelatin in deep 7-inch non-aluminum bowl. Add boiling water; stir until gelatin is completely dissolved.

2. Refrigerate 1 to 2 hours or until partially set.

3. Meanwhile, cut apple crosswise into rounds about $^1/_8$ inch thick. Cut each round into star shapes with cookie cutter. Cut scraps into crescent shapes to resemble moons.

4. Place apple pieces in glass bowl; sprinkle with juice. Cover with plastic wrap and refrigerate until needed.

5. When gelatin is partially set, gently press apple pieces and half of blueberries into gelatin in random fashion. Cover bowl with plastic wrap; refrigerate 3 to 4 hours or until firm.

6. To remove gelatin from bowl, place bowl briefly in pan of hot water. (If necessary, loosen edge of gelatin from pan with narrow spatula.) Invert mold onto serving platter. Arrange oranges and remaining blueberries around outer edge.   *Makes 8 servings*

Incredible Edible Fortune Teller's Ball

Fish Biters

24 giant goldfish-shaped crackers
12 slices pepperoni, halved
12 Monterey Jack cheese cubes, halved
24 small black olive slices
24 flat leaf parsley leaves

1. Preheat oven to 425°F. Coat baking sheet with nonstick cooking spray. Place crackers on prepared baking sheet. Place 2 pepperoni halves on tail ends. Place cheese half in center of each fish.

2. Bake 3 minutes or until cheese is melted. Remove from oven and immediately top with olive slice to resemble eye. Lift up olive slice slightly and place a parsley leaf behind it to resemble fin. Gently press down on olive to adhere. Serve warm. *Makes 24 cracker.*

Monster Munch

6 squares (2 ounces each) almond bark, divided
1¹/₂ cups pretzel sticks
    Orange food coloring
2 cups graham cereal
³/₄ cup Halloween colored candy-coated chocolate pieces
³/₄ cup mini marshmallows
¹/₂ cup chocolate sprinkles

1. Place 1¹/₂ squares almond bark in small microwavable bowl. Microwave on MEDIUM (50%) 1 minute; stir. Repeat as necessary, stirring at 15-second intervals until completely melted.

2. Place pretzel sticks in large bowl. Add melted almond bark and stir until all pieces are coated. Spread coated pretzel sticks out on waxed paper, separating individual pieces; let set.

3. Place remaining 4¹/₂ squares almond bark in medium microwavable bowl. Microwave on MEDIUM (50%) 1 minute; stir. Repeat as necessary, stirring at 15-second intervals until completely melted. Stir in food coloring until almond bark is bright orange.

4. Place cereal in large bowl. Add half of orange-colored almond bark and stir until cereal is evenly coated. Add chocolate pieces, marshmallows and remaining almond bark; stir until mix is evenly coated. Stir in pretzel sticks. Break mix into small clusters and spread out on waxed paper. Sprinkle clusters with chocolate sprinkles; let set. *Makes about 5 cups snack m*

Ghostly Delights

    1 package (18 ounces) refrigerated cookie dough, any flavor
    1 cup prepared vanilla frosting
    $^3/_4$ cup marshmallow creme
    32 chocolate chips
        Halloween sprinkles (optional)

1. Preheat oven to 350°F. Using about 1 tablespoon dough for body and about 1 teaspoon dough for head, form cookie dough into ghost shapes on greased cookie sheets. Bake 10 to 11 minutes or until browned. Cool 1 minute on cookie sheets; place warm cookies on serving plates.

2. While cookies are baking, combine frosting and marshmallow creme in small bowl until well blended.

3. Frost each ghost with frosting mixture. Press 2 chocolate chips, points up, into frosting to create eyes. Decorate with sprinkles, if desired.

Makes 16 servings

Serving Suggestion: These cookies are excellent served with a tall glass of cold milk

Prep and Cook Time: 25 minutes

Cauldron Dipped Apples

8 to 10 medium apples, stems removed
8 to 10 wooden ice cream sticks
PEANUT BUTTER SUGAR (recipe follows)
2 cups (12-ounce package) HERSHEY'S SPECIAL DARK® Chocolate
    Chips or HERSHEY'S Semi-Sweet Chocolate Chips
$1/4$ cup shortening (do not use butter, margarine, spread or oil)
$2/3$ cup REESE'S® Creamy Peanut Butter
$2/3$ cup powdered sugar

1. Line tray with wax paper. Wash and dry apples; insert wooden stick into stem end of each apple.

2. Prepare Peanut Butter Sugar.

3. Melt chocolate chips and shortening in medium saucepan over low heat. Remove from heat. Add peanut butter; stir until melted and smooth. With whisk, blend in powdered sugar.

4. Dip apples into chocolate mixture; twirl gently to remove excess. Sprinkle Peanut Butter Sugar over apples. Place on prepared tray. Refrigerate until coating is firm. Store in refrigerator.   *Makes 8 to 10 dipped apple*

Peanut Butter Sugar

3 tablespoons REESE'S® Creamy Peanut Butter
$1/3$ cup powdered sugar
1 tablespoon granulated sugar

Combine all ingredients in small bowl.   *Makes about $2/3$ cu*

Cauldron Dipped Apples

Mummy Cakes

1 package (about 18 ounces) chocolate cake mix, plus ingredients to
   prepare mix
1/4 cup unsweetened cocoa powder
1 teaspoon ground cinnamon
1 teaspoon ground ginger
1 package (18 ounces) refrigerated sugar cookie dough, room
   temperature
  3-inch gingerbread man cookie cutter

FROSTING & FINISHING

4 cups powdered sugar
1/3 cup plus 1 tablespoon milk
2 teaspoons butter or margarine, softened
48 small red cinnamon candies
3 tablespoons unsweetened cocoa powder
1/2 cup chocolate cookie crumbs

1. Preheat oven to 350°F. Prepare cake mix according to package directions.
Spoon batter into prepared muffin cups, filling two-thirds full. Bake cupcakes
according to package directions. Cool completely and set aside. Line cookie
sheets with parchment paper.

2. Beat 1/4 cup cocoa powder, cinnamon and ginger into cookie dough in
large bowl until well blended. Roll out dough on lightly floured work surface
to 1/4-inch thickness. Cut out cookies using gingerbread man cookie cutter.
Bake on prepared cookie sheets about 7 minutes or until edges are set and no
longer shiny. Cool completely.

3. Beat powdered sugar, milk and butter in large bowl with electric mixer
on medium speed until smooth and creamy. Spoon about one third frosting
into medium resealable food storage bag. Seal bag and snip 1/8 inch from one
corner. Squeeze 2 small dabs frosting onto face of each cookie; top with 2 red
candies to create eyes. Drizzle frosting back and forth over cookie to create
mummy wrappings. Repeat with remaining cookies, frosting and candies; set
aside for frosting to harden.

4. Blend 3 tablespoons cocoa powder into remaining frosting. Spread about
1 tablespoon frosting over each cupcake. Sprinkle 1 teaspoon cookie crumbs
over frosting. Gently push mummy cookies into cupcakes. *Makes 24 cupcakes*

Mummy Cakes

Squished and Squirmy Sandwiches

1 package (9 ounces) vanilla confetti cake mix
$^1/_3$ cup vegetable oil
2 eggs
   Multicolored sprinkles
2 pints vanilla ice cream
32 gummy worms

1. Preheat oven to 375°F.

2. Combine cake mix, oil and eggs in large bowl until well moistened. Shape dough into 32 equal balls. Place 2 inches apart onto ungreased cookie sheets. Gently flatten dough to $^1/_4$-inch thickness. Top with sprinkles.

3. Bake 6 to 8 minutes or until edges are light golden brown. Cool 1 minute on cookie sheets. Remove to wire racks; cool completely.

4. Working quickly, place 2 tablespoons ice cream on flat side of 1 cookie and top with gummy worm, allowing worm to stick out as much as possible. Top with 2 tablespoons ice cream and another worm. Top with another cookie, flat side down, pressing down to flatten slightly. Wrap in foil and freeze. Repeat with remaining cookies, ice cream and gummy worms.

Makes 16 sandwiches

Squished and Squirmy Sandwiches

Monster Pops

1²/₃ cups all-purpose flour
1 teaspoon baking soda
¹/₂ teaspoon salt
1 cup (2 sticks) butter or margarine, softened
³/₄ cup granulated sugar
³/₄ cup packed brown sugar
2 teaspoons vanilla extract
2 eggs
2 cups (12-ounce package) NESTLÉ® TOLL HOUSE® Semi-Sweet Chocolate Morsels
2 cups quick or old-fashioned oats
1 cup raisins
About 24 wooden craft sticks
1 container (16 ounces) prepared vanilla frosting, colored as desired, or colored icing in tubes
Colored candies (such as WONKA® RUNTS and/or NERDS)

PREHEAT oven to 325°F.

COMBINE flour, baking soda and salt in small bowl. Beat butter, granulated sugar, brown sugar and vanilla extract in large mixer bowl until creamy. Beat in eggs. Gradually beat in flour mixture. Stir in morsels, oats and raisins. Drop dough by level ¹/₄-cup measure 3 inches apart onto ungreased baking sheets. Shape into round mounds. Insert wooden stick into each mound.

BAKE for 14 to 18 minutes or until golden brown. Cool on baking sheets on wire racks for 2 minutes; remove to wire racks to cool completely.

DECORATE pops as desired.   *Makes about 2 dozen cookies*

For Speedy Monster Pops: **SUBSTITUTE** 2 packages (16.5 ounce each) NESTLÉ® TOLL HOUSE® Refrigerated Chocolate Chip Cookie Dough for the first nine ingredients, adding 1 cup quick or old-fashioned oats and ¹/₂ cup raisins to the dough. Bake as stated above for 16 to 20 minutes or until golden brown. Makes 1¹/₂ dozen cookies.

Monster Pops

Autumn Leaves

1½ cups (3 sticks) unsalted butter, softened
¾ cup packed light brown sugar
½ teaspoon vanilla
3½ cups all-purpose flour
1 teaspoon ground cinnamon
½ teaspoon salt
⅛ teaspoon ground ginger
⅛ teaspoon ground cloves
2 tablespoons unsweetened cocoa powder
Yellow, orange and red food coloring
⅓ cup semisweet chocolate chips

1. Beat butter, brown sugar and vanilla in large bowl with electric mixer at medium speed until light and fluffy. Add flour, cinnamon, salt, ginger and cloves; beat at low speed until well blended.

2. Divide dough into 5 equal sections. Stir cocoa into 1 section until well blended. (If dough is too dry and will not hold together, add 1 teaspoon water; beat until well blended and dough forms ball.) Stir yellow food coloring into 1 section until well blended and desired shade is reached. Repeat with 2 sections and orange and red food colorings. Leave remaining section plain.

3. Preheat oven to 350°F. Lightly grease cookie sheets. Working with half of each dough color, press colors together lightly. Roll dough on lightly floured surface to ¼-inch thickness. Cut dough with leaf-shaped cookie cutters of various shapes and sizes. Place similarly sized cutouts 2 inches apart on prepared cookie sheets. Repeat with remaining dough and scraps.

4. Bake 10 to 15 minutes or until edges are lightly browned. Remove to wire racks; cool completely.

5. Place chocolate chips in small resealable food storage bag; seal. Microwave on HIGH 1 minute; knead bag lightly. Microwave on HIGH for additional 30-second intervals until chips are completely melted, kneading bag after each interval. Cut off tiny corner of bag. Pipe chocolate onto cookies in vein patterns. *Makes about 2 dozen cookies*

Spider Cupcakes

1 package (about 18 ounces) yellow or white cake mix
1 cup solid-pack pumpkin
¾ cup water
3 eggs
2 tablespoons vegetable oil
1 teaspoon ground cinnamon
1 teaspoon pumpkin pie spice*
  Orange food coloring
1 container (16 ounces) vanilla, cream cheese or caramel frosting
4 squares (1 ounce each) semisweet chocolate
48 black gumdrops

*Or substitute ½ teaspoon ground cinnamon, ¼ teaspoon ground ginger and ⅛ teaspoon each ground allspice and ground nutmeg for 1 teaspoon pumpkin pie spice.

1. Preheat oven to 350°F. Line 24 standard (2½-inch) muffin cups with paper baking cups or spray with nonstick cooking spray.

2. Beat cake mix, pumpkin, water, eggs, oil, cinnamon and pumpkin pie spice in large bowl with electric mixer at medium speed 3 minutes or until well blended. Spoon ¼ cup batter into each prepared muffin cup.

3. Bake about 20 minutes or until toothpick inserted into centers comes out clean. Cool cupcakes in pans 10 minutes. Remove to wire racks; cool completely.

4. Stir food coloring into frosting in small bowl until desired share of orange is reached. Frost cupcakes.

5. Place chocolate in small resealable food storage bag. Microwave on MEDIUM (50%) 40 seconds. Knead bag; microwave 30 seconds to 1 minute or until chocolate is melted and smooth. Cut off tiny corner of bag. Pipe chocolate in four or five concentric circles over frosting. Immediately draw 5 to 8 lines at regular intervals from center to edges of cupcakes with toothpick or knife to create web.

6. Place one gumdrop in center of web. Roll out another gumdrop on generously sugared surface. Slice thinly and roll for legs; arrange around gumdrop to create spiders. 　　　　　　　　　　　　　*Makes 24 cupcakes*

Graveyard Pudding Dessert

3½ cups cold milk
2 packages (4-serving size) JELL-O® Chocolate Flavor Instant
    Pudding & Pie Filling
1 tub (12 ounces) COOL WHIP® Whipped Topping, thawed
1 package (16 ounces) chocolate sandwich cookies, crushed
    Decorations: assorted rectangular-shaped sandwich cookies,
    decorator icings, candy corn and pumpkins

POUR milk into large bowl. Add pudding mixes. Beat with wire whisk or electric mixer on lowest speed 2 minutes or until blended. Gently stir in whipped topping and ½ of the crushed cookies. Spoon into 13×9-inch dish. Sprinkle with remaining crushed cookies.

REFRIGERATE 1 hour or until ready to serve. Decorate rectangular-shaped sandwich cookies with icings to make "tombstones." Stand tombstones on top of dessert with candies to resemble a graveyard.   *Makes 15 servings*

Prep Time: 15 minutes | Chill Time: 1 hour

Graveyard Pudding Dessert

People Chow

1 package (12 ounces) semisweet chocolate chips
1 cup (2 sticks) butter or margarine
18 cups dry cereal (mixture of bite-size wheat, corn and rice cereal
     squares or toasted oat cereal)
2 cups mixed nuts
6 cups powdered sugar
1 cup mini marshmallows
     Black decorating gel

Melt chocolate chips and butter in heavy medium saucepan over low heat; cook and stir until melted and smooth. Place cereal and nuts in very large bowl. Pour chocolate mixture over cereal and nuts; mix until thoroughly coated. Sprinkle with sugar, 2 cups at a time, carefully folding and mixing until thoroughly coated. Decorate marshmallows with black gel faces; add to mix.

Makes about 24 cups

Fishy Squishy Squirters

20 brightly colored fruit leather rolls
40 seedless red or green grapes, rinsed and patted dry
     Black decorating gel
20 red hot candies

1. Unwrap one piece of fruit leather and place on clean work surface.

2. Arrange 2 grapes, end to end lengthwise, about 1 inch from one corner. Fold nearest corner over grapes; wrap sides in to cover fold and form triangle. Pinch fruit leather together at base of grapes to make tail. Place on waxed paper-lined plate and repeat with remaining grapes and fruit leathers. Shape tails to fan out.

3. Place two large dots of decorating gel on each fish to form base for eyes. Place red hot candy on each dot. Loosely cover with plastic wrap and store in cool dry place until ready to serve.

Makes 20 fish

 TIP: For a variation, use mini candy-coated plain chocolate candy pieces instead of red hot candies for fish eyes.

People Chow

Trick or Treat Ice Cream Sandwiches

$^1/_2$ cup (1 stick) butter, softened
$^3/_4$ cup granulated sugar
$^3/_4$ cup packed light brown sugar
3 egg whites
1 teaspoon vanilla
$2^1/_2$ cups all-purpose flour
$1^1/_2$ teaspoons baking soda
1 teaspoon ground cinnamon
$^1/_2$ teaspoon salt
1 package (6 ounces) semisweet chocolate chips
$1^1/_2$ cups orange sherbet, slightly softened

1. Preheat oven to 350°F. Spray cookie sheets with nonstick cooking spray; set aside.

2. Beat butter in large bowl until creamy. Add sugars; beat until fluffy. Blend in egg whites and vanilla. Combine flour, baking soda, cinnamon and salt in medium bowl. Add to butter mixture; mix until well blended. Stir in chocolate chips.

3. Drop cookie dough by heaping teaspoonfuls onto prepared cookie sheets, making 48 cookies. Bake until cookies are lightly browned, 10 to 12 minutes. Remove to wire racks; cool completely.

4. For each sandwich, place 1 tablespoon sherbet on flat side of 1 cookie; top with second cookie, flat side down. Press cookies together gently to even out sherbet layer. Repeat with remaining cookies and sherbet. Wrap tightly and store in freezer. *Makes 2 dozen sandwich cookies*

Goblin Ice Cream Sandwiches: Prepare and freeze cookie sandwiches as directed. Just before serving, decorate 1 side of sandwich with Halloween candies or decorating gel to resemble goblin faces.

Colossal Cookie Sandwich: Prepare dough as directed. Substitute 2 lightly greased foil-lined 12-inch pizza pans for cookie sheets. Substitute 1 quart (4 cups) frozen yogurt or ice cream for $1^1/_2$ cups orange sherbet. Prepare cookie dough as directed; divide evenly in half. Spread each half evenly onto bottom of prepared pizza pan to within $^1/_2$ inch of outer edge. Bake until cookies are lightly browned, 10 to 15 minutes. Cool cookies in pans just until cookies begin to firm; slide onto wire racks to cool completely. Spoon yogurt onto flat side of 1 cookie. Top with remaining cookie, flat side down. Freeze until yogurt is firm, about 6 hours. Cut into wedges to serve. Makes 24 servings.

Trick or Treat Ice Cream Sandwiches

Treasure Chests

1 package (about 19 ounces) brownie mix, plus ingredients to
   prepare mix
1 container (16 ounces) chocolate frosting
24 fudge-covered graham crackers
   Yellow decorating icing
   Mini candy-coated chocolate pieces
   Yellow decorating gel

1. Preheat oven to 350°F. Coat 9-inch square baking pan with nonstick cooking spray.

2. Prepare brownie mix according to package directions; pour batter into prepared pan. Bake 35 minutes or until toothpick inserted into center comes out clean. Cool completely in pan on wire rack. Cover; freeze 1 hour or overnight.

3. Run knife around edges of brownies. Place cutting board over baking pan; invert and let stand until brownies release from pan. Trim edges; discard. Cut into 24 rectangles.

4. Spread tops and sides of brownies with frosting. Let stand on wire racks 10 minutes or until set. Pipe lines on brownies and graham crackers with decorating icing to resemble chests.

5. Dot back of chocolate pieces with decorating gel; adhere on front half of brownie tops for treasure. Spread 1 edge of each graham cracker with frosting; adhere 1 graham cracker to back half of each brownie top so that it leans on chocolate pieces. Let stand 10 minutes or until set.

Makes 2 dozen brownies

Great Pumpkin Cake

1 package (2 layer) cake mix, any flavor
1 package (8 ounces) PHILADELPHIA® Cream Cheese, softened
1/4 cup (1/2 stick) butter, softened
4 cups powdered sugar
Few drops each: green, red and yellow food coloring
1 COMET® Ice Cream Cone

1. Prepare cake batter and bake in 12-cup fluted tube pan as directed on package. Cool in pan 10 minutes Invert cake onto wire rack; remove pan. Cool cake completely.

2. Meanwhile, beat cream cheese and butter in medium bowl with electric mixer on medium speed until blended. Gradually add sugar, beating until well blended after each addition. Remove 1/2 cup of the frosting; place in small bowl. Add green food coloring; stir until well blended. Spread half of the green frosting onto outside of ice cream cone; set aside. Cover and reserve remaining green frosting for later use.

3. Add red and yellow food colorings to remaining white frosting to tint it orange. Spread onto cake to resemble pumpkin. Invert ice cream cone in hole in top of cake for the pumpkin's stem. Pipe the reserved green frosting in vertical lines down side of cake. *24 servings, 1 slice each*

Cooking Know-How: For a more rounded Great Pumpkin Cake, use a tall 12-cup fluted tube pan. As the cake bakes, it rises and forms a rounded top. When cake is unmolded (upside-down), the bottom of the cake will be rounded. If the cake is baked in a shorter 12-cup fluted tube pan, the resulting cake will be flatter.

Fun Idea: Place black gumdrops on sheet of waxed paper sprinkled with additional granulated sugar. Use a rolling pin to flatter each gumdrop, turning frequently to coat both sides with sugar. Cut into desired shapes with a sharp knife. Use to decorated frosted cake to resemble a jack-o'-lantern.

Prep Time: 30 minutes | Bake Time: as directed

Pumpkin White Chocolate Drops

2 cups granulated sugar
2 cups (4 sticks) butter, softened
1 can (about 16 ounces) solid-pack pumpkin
2 eggs
4 cups all-purpose flour
2 teaspoons pumpkin pie spice*
1 teaspoon baking powder
$^1/_2$ teaspoon baking soda
1 package (12 ounces) white chocolate chips
1 container (16 ounces) cream cheese frosting
$^1/_4$ cup packed brown sugar

Substitute 1 teaspoon ground cinnamon, $^1/_2$ teaspoon ground ginger, $^1/_4$ teaspoon ground allspice and $^1/_4$ teaspoon ground nutmeg for 2 teaspoons pumpkin pie spice.

1. Preheat oven to 375°F. Grease cookie sheets.

2. Beat granulated sugar and butter in large bowl with electric mixer at medium speed until light and fluffy. Add pumpkin and eggs; beat until well blended. Add flour, pumpkin pie spice, baking powder and baking soda; beat just until blended. Stir in white chocolate chips.

3. Drop dough by teaspoonfuls about 2 inches apart onto prepared cookie sheets. Bake 16 minutes or until set and lightly browned. Cool on cookie sheets 1 minute. Remove to wire racks; cool completely.

4. Combine frosting and brown sugar in small bowl. Spread on warm cookies.

Makes about 6 dozen cookies

Pumpkin White Chocolate Drops

Pumpkin Ice Cream Pie with Caramel Sauce

25 gingersnap cookies, finely crushed (about 1$\frac{1}{2}$ cups)
$\frac{1}{4}$ cup ($\frac{1}{2}$ stick) butter, melted
2 tablespoons granulated sugar
4 cups pumpkin ice cream, softened (about 1 quart)
1 cup pecan halves, toasted*

CARAMEL SAUCE
1 cup packed dark brown sugar
$\frac{1}{2}$ cup whipping cream
6 tablespoons ($\frac{3}{4}$ stick) unsalted butter
$\frac{1}{4}$ cup light corn syrup
$\frac{1}{2}$ teaspoon salt

*To toast pecans, spread them on a baking sheet and place in a preheated 350°F oven for 8 to 10 minutes.

1. Preheat oven to 350°F. Coat 9-inch pie plate with nonstick cooking spray.

2. For crust, combine cookie crumbs, melted butter and granulated sugar; mix well. Press onto bottom and side of prepared pie plate. Bake 8 minutes. Cool completely on wire rack.

3. Fill crust with ice cream; smooth top. Cover and freeze 1 hour.

4. For sauce, whisk brown sugar, cream, 6 tablespoons butter, corn syrup and salt in medium saucepan over medium-high heat until sugar dissolves and mixture comes to a boil. Reduce heat; boil 1 minute without stirring. Remove from heat and cool.

5. Cut pie into wedges; top with caramel sauce and pecans.

Makes 8 servings

Pumpkin Ice Cream Pie with Caramel Sauce

Spider Web Pumpkin Cheesecake

18 OREO® Chocolate Sandwich Cookies, finely crushed (about 1¹/₂ cups)
 2 tablespoons butter or margarine, melted
 3 packages (8 ounces each) PHILADELPHIA® Cream Cheese, softened
³/₄ cup sugar
 1 can (15 ounces) pumpkin
 1 tablespoon pumpkin pie spice
 3 eggs
 1 cup BREAKSTONE'S® or KNUDSEN® Sour Cream
 1 square BAKER'S® Semi-Sweet Baking Chocolate
 1 teaspoon butter or margarine

1. Preheat oven to 350°F if using a silver 9-inch springform pan (or 325°F if using a dark 9-inch nonstick springform pan). Mix cookie crumbs and 2 tablespoons butter; press firmly onto bottom of pan. Set aside.

2. Beat cream cheese and sugar in large bowl with electric mixer on medium speed until well blended. Add pumpkin and pumpkin pie spice, mix well. Add eggs, one at a time, mixing on low speed after each addition just until blended. Pour over crust.

3. Bake 50 to 55 minutes or until center is almost set; cool slightly. Carefully spread sour cream over top of cheesecake. Run knife or metal spatula around rim of pan to loosen cheesecake; cool before removing rim of pan.

4. Place chocolate and 1 teaspoon butter in small microwave bowl. Microwave on MEDIUM (50%) 30 seconds; stir until chocolate is completely melted. Drizzle over cheesecake in spiral pattern. Starting at center of cheesecake, pull a toothpick through lines from center of cheesecake to outside edge of cheesecake to resemble a spider's web. Refrigerate 4 hours or overnight. Store leftover cheesecake in refrigerator.   *Make 16 servings*

Make It Easy: For easy drizzling, pour melted chocolate into small plastic bag. Snip off a small piece from one of the bottom corners of the bag. Gently squeeze bag to drizzle chocolate over cheesecake as directed.

Prep Time: 15 minutes plus refrigerating | Bake Time: 55 minutes

Spider Web Pumpkin Cheesecake

Jack-O'-Lantern

2 recipes Buttercream Frosting (recipe follows)
Orange, green and brown food colorings
2 (10-inch) bundt cakes
Base Frosting (page 78)
1 (6-ounce) ice cream wafer cone
Candy corn

SUPPLIES

2 (10-inch) round cake boards, stacked and covered, or large plate
Pastry bag and medium writing tip

1. Prepare Buttercream Frosting. Tint $4\frac{1}{2}$ cups frosting orange, $\frac{1}{2}$ cup dark green and $\frac{1}{4}$ cup dark brown. To tint frosting, add small amount of desired coloring; stir well. Slowly add more coloring until frosting is desired shade.

2. Trim flat sides of cakes. Place one cake on prepared cake board, flat side up. Frost top of cake with thin coat of orange frosting. Place second cake, flat side down, over frosting.

3. Prepare Base Frosting. Frost entire cake with Base Frosting to seal in crumbs. Frost again with remaining orange frosting.

4. Frost cone with green frosting. Place upside-down in center of cake for stem. Touch up frosting, if necessary.

5. Pipe eyes and mouth using writing tip and brown frosting. Arrange candy corn for teeth as shown in photo. Slice and serve top cake first, then bottom.

Makes 36 to 40 servings

Buttercream Frosting

6 cups powdered sugar, sifted and divided
$\frac{3}{4}$ cup ($1\frac{1}{2}$ sticks) butter, softened
$\frac{1}{4}$ cup shortening
6 to 8 tablespoons milk, divided
1 teaspoon vanilla

Beat 3 cups powdered sugar, butter, shortening, 4 tablespoons milk and vanilla in large bowl with electric mixer at low speed until smooth. Add remaining 3 cups powdered sugar; beat until light and fluffy, adding more milk, 1 tablespoon at a time, as needed for good spreading consistency.

Makes about $3\frac{1}{2}$ cups

continued on page 80

Jack-O'-Lantern

Jack-O'-Lantern, continued

Base Frosting

3 cups powdered sugar, sifted
$^1/_2$ cup shortening
$^1/_4$ cup milk
$^1/_2$ teaspoon vanilla
Additional milk

Beat powdered sugar, shortening, $^1/_4$ cup milk and vanilla in large bowl with electric mixer at low speed until smooth. Add more milk, 1 teaspoon at a time, until frosting is thin consistency. Use frosting immediately.

Makes about 2 cups

Pumpkin Chocolate Chip Muffins

$2^1/_2$ cups all-purpose flour
1 tablespoon baking powder
$1^1/_2$ teaspoons pumpkin pie spice*
$^1/_2$ teaspoon salt
1 cup solid-pack pumpkin
1 cup packed light brown sugar
$^3/_4$ cup milk
6 tablespoons ($^3/_4$ stick) butter, melted
2 eggs
1 cup semisweet chocolate chips
$^1/_2$ cup chopped walnuts

Or substitute $^3/_4$ teaspoon ground cinnamon, $^1/_2$ teaspoon ground ginger and $^1/_4$ teaspoon each ground allspice and ground nutmeg.

1. Preheat oven to 400°F. Line 18 standard (2$^1/_2$-inch) muffin cups with paper baking cups or spray with nonstick cooking spray.

2. Combine flour, baking powder, pumpkin pie spice and salt in large bowl. Beat pumpkin, brown sugar, milk, butter and eggs in medium bowl until well blended. Add pumpkin mixture, chocolate chips and walnuts to flour mixture; stir just until moistened. Spoon evenly into prepared muffin cups, filling two-thirds full.

3. Bake 15 to 17 minutes or until toothpick inserted into centers comes out clean. Cool 10 minutes in pans on wire racks. Remove from pans; cool completely.

Makes 18 muffin.

Pumpkin Chocolate Chip Muffins

Hot Cocoa with Floating Eyeballs

INGREDIENTS

 16 large marshmallows
 16 black licorice candies
  2 quarts milk
  1 cup chocolate drink mix
  1 cup mint semisweet chocolate chips

SUPPLIES

 16 lollipop sticks

1. Make slit in center of each marshmallow; insert licorice candy into slit. Insert lollipop stick into center of bottom of each eyeball; set aside.

2. Combine milk and drink mix in medium saucepan. Stir in chocolate chips. Cook and stir over medium heat until chips are melted and milk is heated through.

3. Place 2 eyeballs in each mug; fill mug with hot cocoa. Serve immediately.

Makes 8 servings

Variation: Omit sticks and float marshmallows in hot cocoa.

Magic Potion

Creepy Crawler Ice Ring (recipe follows)
1 cup boiling water
2 packages (4-serving size each) lime gelatin
3 cups cold water
1 1/2 liters (48 ounces) lemon-lime soda, chilled
1/2 cup granulated sugar
Gummy worms (optional)

1. Prepare Creepy Crawler Ice Ring one day before serving.

2. Pour boiling water over gelatin in heatproof punch bowl; stir until gelatin dissolves. Stir in cold water. Add lemon-lime soda and sugar; stir well (mixture will foam for several minutes).

3. Before serving, unmold ice ring by dipping bottom of mold briefly into hot water; add to punch bowl. Serve cups of punch garnished with gummy worms, if desired. *Makes about 10 servings*

Haunted Hint: This Magic Potion can easily go from creepy to cute. For the punch, use orange-flavored gelatin instead of lime. For the ice ring, use candy corn and candy pumpkins instead of gummy worms.

Creepy Crawler Ice Ring

1 cup gummy worms or other creepy crawler candy
1 quart lemon-lime thirst quencher beverage

Arrange gummy worms in bottom of 5-cup ring mold or bowl; fill mold with thirst quencher beverage. Freeze until solid, 8 hours or overnight.
Makes 1 ice ring

Magic Potion

Voodoo Juice

　1 cup distilled water, divided
12 whole strawberries
24 fresh or frozen blueberries
12 mandarin orange sections
　8 cups chilled fruit punch, apple cider or favorite soft drink

1. Place 1 tablespoon water in each of 12 mini (1³/₄-inch) muffin cups. Freeze 1 hour or until frozen solid.

2. Slice ¹/₄-inch off pointed end of each strawberry. Arrange 2 blueberries at top of each cup of ice for eyes, 1 strawberry tip pointed up in center for nose and 1 orange section directly under strawberry tip for smile.

3. Spoon teaspoon of remaining water over each; freeze 2 hours or until frozen solid.

4. At serving time, remove ice by placing back of muffin pan in larger pan of water until faces release.

5. Pour chilled punch into small glasses. Place 1 frozen face in each glass. The water will gradually melt around the fruit, causing the faces to shrink and disappear! *Makes 12 servings*

 TIP: Frozen faces may be made up to 48 hours in advance.

Voodoo Juice

Creamy Crypt Coolers

2 cups vanilla ice cream
2 cups orange sherbet
2 cups orange juice
5 drops yellow food coloring
5 drops red food coloring
1 cup lemon-lime soda

1. Combine ice cream, sherbet, juice and food coloring in blender. Process until smooth.

2. Add soda. Process until just blended. Serve immediately.   *Makes 5 cups*

Witches' Brew

2 cups apple cider
$1^1/_2$ to 2 cups vanilla ice cream
2 tablespoons honey
$^1/_2$ teaspoon ground cinnamon
$^1/_4$ teaspoon ground nutmeg

1. Process cider, ice cream, honey, cinnamon and nutmeg in food processor or blender until smooth.

2. Pour into glasses and sprinkle with additional nutmeg. Serve immediately.

 Makes 4 servings

Serving Suggestion: Add a few drops of desired food coloring to ingredients in food processor to make a scary brew.

Prep Time: 10 minutes

 TIP: Serve in creepy, Halloween-themed cups with spooky straws.

Creamy Crypt Coolers

Trick-or-Treat Punch

Green food coloring (optional)
1 can (12 ounces) frozen lemonade concentrate, thawed
1 envelope (4 ounces) orange presweetened drink mix
1 bottle (2 liters) ginger ale*
1 can (12 ounces) sparkling water or soda, cold

SUPPLIES
1 new plastic food-safe glove

For an adult party, substitute 2 bottles (750 ml each) champagne for ginger ale, if desired.

1. One day ahead, fill pitcher with 3 cups water; tint with green food coloring, if desired. Pour into glove; tightly secure wrist of glove with twist tie. Line baking sheet with paper towels; place glove on prepared baking sheet. Use inverted custard cup to elevate tied end of glove to prevent leaking. Freeze overnight.

2. When ready to serve, combine lemonade concentrate, 4 cups water and drink mix in punch bowl; stir until drink mix is dissolved and mixture is well blended. Stir in ginger ale and sparkling water.

3. Cut glove away from ice; float frozen hand in punch. *Makes 16 servings*

Bloody Blast

3 cans (12 ounces each) tomato or vegetable juice
2 tablespoons Worcestershire sauce
1 tablespoon prepared horseradish
1 tablespoon lemon juice
$1/4$ to $1/2$ teaspoon hot pepper sauce
Celery ribs and olives (optional)

1. Combine tomato juice, Worcestershire, horseradish, lemon juice and hot pepper sauce in pitcher. Chill at least 1 hour.

2. Pour into ice-filled glasses. Garnish with celery stalks and olives for eyes, if desired. *Makes 6 servings*

Trick-or-Treat Punch

Candy Corn Shots

Decorative sugar in yellow, orange and white
1 to 3 tubes (0.6 ounces each) decorating gel
   (white, yellow and/or orange)
4 to 6 clear shot glasses
2 large scoops orange sherbet (about 1 cup)
1 cup milk
2 tablespoons frozen orange juice concentrate

1. Place decorative sprinkles in a small bowl. (You can mix colors together or keep them separate.) Squeeze gel along rim of each glass and dip into sugar; set aside.

2. Process sherbet, milk and orange juice concentrate in blender about 1 minute or until smooth. Pour into prepared glasses. Serve immediately.

Makes 4 to 6 servings

 TIP: For a fun accompaniment, serve with cream-filled rolled wafer cookies covered with gel and dipped in sprinkles.

Candy Corn Shots

Spooky Crafts

Haunted Hat Snapshot Holder

A pinch of this, a handful of that and POOF! You'll be spellbound at the simplicity
of this handy hat, which is perfect for holding photos, recipes or magical messages.

WHAT YOU'LL NEED

- Black modeling clay
- 24 inches copper wire, 20 gauge
- Needle-nose pliers with wire cutter
- 1 foot green iridescent wire ribbon
- Scissors
- Hot glue gun, glue sticks
- 1 gold star button

1. Shape clay into hat by making 4-inch circle for base and 4-inch cone for
pointed crown.

2. Combine shapes by pressing black cone firmly onto round base. Gently pull
tip of cone over to one side; mold into drooping point. Slightly turn up edges
of base on opposite side to create an upturned brim. Let harden for at least
8 hours.

3. Cut 2 pieces of wire: one 15 inches
and one 9 inches. Use pliers to grasp one
end of wire; gently curve it to create
swirl. Repeat on second wire. Stick sharp
ends of wires into side of hat.

4. Hot-glue ribbon where cone meets
base of hat. Cut off excess ribbon;
hot-glue star on the ribbon at front
of hat.

Dare to Drink Coasters

Park those scary drinks on these festive and spooky coasters!

WHAT YOU'LL NEED

- Scissors
- Cork
- Measuring tape
- Felt squares: fluorescent green, black, white, purple, orange
- Pencil
- Embroidery needle
- Embroidery floss: white, black
- Fabric glue
- Assorted sequins
- $^3/_8$-inch grosgrain ribbon with white zigzag stitch
- Cardstock alphabet stickers
- Assorted flat-back buttons
- Tulle

1. Cut cork into four $3^1/_4$-inch squares. Cut eight $3^1/_2$-inch felt squares. For top frame, cut out a 3-inch diameter circle from 4 felt squares.

2. Cut out $1^3/_8$-inch circles for cat and goblin, $1^1/_2 \times 1^3/_4$-inch rectangle for Frankenstein and 2-inch wide pumpkin. Cut out detail shapes. Use needle and floss to blanket-stitch around heads. Use fabric glue to attach sequins and details to faces. Glue 1-inch ribbon lengths for mouths.

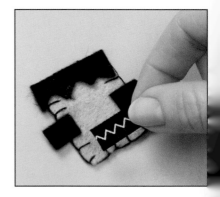

3. Using frames as guides for placement, glue faces to $3^1/_2$-inch felt squares. Sew cat whiskers with needle and white embroidery floss. Attach alphabet stickers to background felt.

4. Use embroidery needle and thread to blanket-stitch around edges of frames. Sew buttons in corners. Cut four $3^1/_4$-inch squares from tulle.

5. With fabric glue, attach background felt to cork. Glue edges of tulle to edges of background felt. Glue felt frame on top of tulle.

Kooky Bones Plate

Spook guests with your wicked talent by painting party plates.
Creating them is so quick and easy, it's scary!

WHAT YOU'LL NEED

- 10-inch clear glass plate
- Scissors
- Masking tape
- Enamel glass paints: licorice-black, wicker white
- Paint tip set: extension cap, super-fine tip
- Disposable plate
- Paintbrushes: #6 flat, medium spouncer sponge

1. Enlarge pattern below to fit plate, make 2 copies and cut them out. Match sides and tape patterns together. Snip ½-inch tabs all around pattern to fit pattern to plate. Position and tape pattern facedown on top of glass plate. Design will be painted on bottom of plate.

2. Attach extension cap and super-fine tip to black enamel bottle. Practice making a few paint lines on disposable plate, then paint outlines of bones. Let dry. (Quickly and thoroughly rinse out cap, metal tip and brushes after use.)

3. Use #6 flat brush to paint bones white. Let dry. Keep all brush strokes going in same direction. If desired, repeat for opaque coverage. Leaving a thin first coat will give the appearance of old bones once the black background is painted.

4. Using spouncer sponge, spounce black over back of plate; cover completely. Repeat with a second coat if needed.

5. Follow manufacturers' instructions on enamel bottles for drying, baking and curing enamel.

Note: Hand wash plates.

Terrifying Tip: Painting mistakes can be removed by washing them with water before the enamel has dried completely. If paint is dry, scrape the dried enamel off with your fingernail. Once the enamel has cured, it becomes permanent.

Kooky Bones Plate, Shrunken Head (page 20)

Halloween Party Bags

Delight each guest with a small Halloween bag of treats.
Long after the goodies are gone, they'll remember what a fun time they had.

WHAT YOU'LL NEED

- Scissors
- Ruler
- Felt sheets: orange, black
- Straight pins
- Sewing machine
- Thread: black, orange
- Black embroidery floss
- Embroidery needle

1. Cut two 6-inch squares and two 3×6-inch rectangles from orange felt. Cut one 3×6-inch rectangle and two 8×1-inch rectangles from black felt.

2. Enlarge and trace jack-o'-lantern pattern onto black felt and cut out. Pin face to a 6-inch orange square. Sew along edges of face pieces with black thread using sewing machine.

3. Using orange thread and a ¼-inch seam allowance, sew the longer side of a 3×6-inch orange rectangle to either side of a 6-inch square. Sew other 6-inch square to the other sides of 3×6-inch rectangles. Pin and sew black 3×6-inch rectangle to create bottom of bag.

Enlarge Pattern 195%

Halloween Party Bags

4. To create handles, fold black 8×1-inch pieces in half. Sew along length with a ⅛-inch seam allowance using black thread. Pin a handle to either side of front panel at the top and pin other handle to either side of back panel. With a ¼-inch seam allowance, sew along top of bag.

5. With embroidery floss, blanket stitch all edges of bag, using seams as guides.

 TIP: Make alternate party bags using different felt colors with ghost and cat patterns below.

Enlarge Pattern 195%

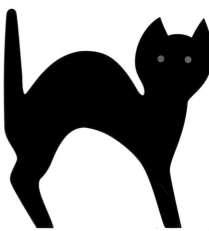

Enlarge Pattern 195%

Tomb Many Days to Count

Count down the days to Halloween on this funny mummy's tummy!

WHAT YOU'LL NEED

- Craft glue
- Craft chipboard (or cereal box)
- Scissors
- 5×7-inch chalkboard
- Batting or stuffing scraps
- 1 yard muslin
- Alphabet rubber stamps
- Stamp pads: antique linen, vintage photo, black soot
- $2^3/_8 \times 4$-inch scrapbook tag
- Hemp cord
- 2 wiggle eyes, 25mm each
- 3 black brads
- Black fine-point marker
- Black 20-gauge wire
- Chalk

1. Glue chipboard together, doubling the thickness. Using patterns on page 102, enlarge, trace and cut out shapes from chipboard.

2. Glue head to top of chalkboard, arms to sides and legs to bottom. Glue batting to chipboard pieces. Let dry.

3. Tear 2-inch strips from muslin. Tie strip ends together to make 1 long strip. Wrap muslin around mummy, covering all chipboard pieces. Glue strips of muslin over wood of chalkboard to cover.

4. Distress mummy with antique linen ink. Distress scrapbook tag with antique linen and vintage photo ink. Stamp words on tag using black soot ink. Tie 2 pieces of hemp cord to tag; attach tag to mummy's arm. Tie knots in hemp.

5. Glue eyes to head. Attach a brad at shoulder, another on leg and another on top of tag. Use marker to make spider legs beside brads. Tie wire around neck; wrap wire around chalk.

Enlarge Pattern 285%

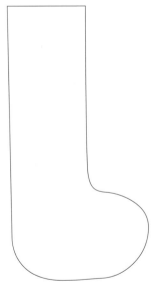

Enlarge Pattern 285%

Enlarge Pattern 285%

Frankenstein Brains

Frankly, it's a delight to serve a delicious concoction in Frankie's head.

WHAT YOU'LL NEED

- 15-ounce clear plastic tumbler
- Blazing red solvent ink
- Watermark stamp pad
- Ultrathick embossing powder
- Heat gun
- Vegetable can
- Measuring tape
- Cardstock: 2 sheets green, black, scrap red
- Scissors
- Glue stick
- Double-sided craft tape
- $\frac{1}{2}$-inch hole punch
- Round-head machine screws with nuts

1. Working on outside of tumbler in a downward motion, use red solvent ink to make a dripping pattern. Let dry. Use stamp pad over red ink; sprinkle on embossing powder. Use heat gun to melt enamel.

2. Measure circumference and height of can. Divide circumference in half; cut 2 pieces of green cardstock that size, adding $1 \times 1\frac{1}{4}$-inch tabs on both sides of cardstock about 2 inches down from top. Cut 2 tongues and 2 scars from red cardstock. Cut hair from black cardstock. Glue pieces to green cardstock.

3. Add tape to back of green cardstock pieces; do not place tape on ear tabs. Peel backing off tape; place pieces on can, butting ear tabs. Punch hole in middle of each ear.

4. Cover all paper with stamp pad and sprinkle on embossing powder. Use heat gun to melt embossing powder.

5. Add screws and nuts to holes in ears. Place tumbler on top of Frankenstein's head. Fill with dip or snack mix.

Frankenstein Brains, Guacamole (page 40)

Ghoulish Glow Candles

Frighteningly fun candles are a great way
to add moody lighting to your Halloween scene.

WHAT YOU'LL NEED

- Scissors
- 4 assorted pillar candles
- Ball-head stylus
- Paintbrush
- Black acrylic paint
- Craft eyelets
- Star brads
- Straight pins
- Colorful ball-head quilting pins
- Wire cutters
- Seed beads

1. Enlarge patterns below and copy to fit candles. Cut out inside of letters to create stencils. Place each stencil on a candle and mark outline with stylus. Use stylus to make groove about $\frac{1}{8}$-inch deep. You may need to do a few passes over letters to get a good groove. Remove stencil. Don't worry if it looks less than spooktacular at this point—paint will cover faults. Use dry paintbrush to brush out shavings from grooves.

2. Paint in letter grooves; let dry. Repeat if necessary.

3. Push eyelets and star brads randomly into candles. Shorten straight and quilting pins with wire cutters so they are about $\frac{1}{2}$ inch long. Randomly push quilting pins into candles. Place seed beads on straight pins and push pins into candles.

Ghoulish Glow Candles

Monster Munchies Treat Jars

Showcase spooky treats with these frightfully fun friends!

WHAT YOU'LL NEED

- Glass jars with black lids
- Polymer clay: silver, bright green, black, red, white
- Strong craft adhesive

1. Size of clay pieces will depend on size of jar. Scale pieces to jar size. Knead polymer clay to condition.

2. For Frankenstein: Make neck knobs from silver clay, ears and nose from bright green. Make eyes from black; add small white dots to eyes. Make mouth and scar from red.

3. For bat: Make ears from black clay; add smaller silver triangles to ears. Make eyes, nose and 2 wings from black (see wing pattern below). Add small white dots to eyes. Make mouth from red and teeth from white. Add silver lines on wings. Wings should have a flat end to attach to jar; remainder of wing should bend out from jar.

4. For Dracula: Make hair triangle and eyes from black clay and nose and teeth from white. Add small white dots to eyes. Make mouth and bow tie from red. Make cape collar from black; make collar one piece that encircles bottom of jar. Add red bow tie to front of collar.

5. Bake clay pieces according to manufacturer's directions; let cool. Attach clay pieces to containers using craft adhesive. Let dry.

6. Fill jars with colored treats and watch them come to life!

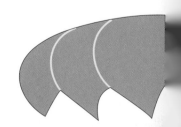

Monster Munchies Treat Jars

Spooky House Centerpiece

A little Halloween magic transforms an ordinary wooden birdhouse into a charismatic cottage with a crooked chimney, spooky bat accents and a glittery black roof.

WHAT YOU'LL NEED

- Wooden birdhouse
- Needle-nose pliers
- Wood filler
- Sandpaper
- Acrylic paint: purple, black, yellow
- 4 foam paintbrushes
- Wooden star cutout
- Pencil or white colored pencil
- Lightweight cardboard or craft foam
- Construction paper: black, blue
- Scissors
- Craft glue
- Black modeling clay
- Hot glue gun, glue sticks
- Copper wire: 18 gauge, 22 gauge
- Wire cutters
- 6 silver star sequins
- Glitter: black, crystal
- Raffia: black, orange
- Floral accent pumpkin

1. If birdhouse has a perch, pull it out using needle-nose pliers. Fill hole with wood filler; let dry. Sand smooth.

2. Paint house purple and roof black. Paint wooden star yellow. Let dry.

3. Draw checkerboard pattern onto lightweight cardboard or craft foam; cut out. Stencil checks around middle of house using black paint. Let dry.

4. Trace the door pattern onto black construction paper; cut out. Use craft glue to glue the door on front of house, covering hole and perch area.

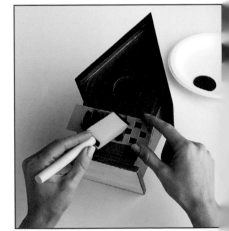

Spooky House Centerpiece

5. Mold crooked chimney out of modeling clay. Let harden for at least 8 hours. Hot-glue chimney to roof.

6. Cut 18-gauge wire into 6-inch length and bend into curved line. Hot-glue this wire to the back of wooden star. Stick other end deep inside chimney to hold in place.

7. Cut 22-gauge wire into 3 pieces, approximately 3 to 4 inches each. Bend into curvy lines. Sandwich one end of wire between 2 silver star sequins and hot-glue 3 pieces together. Repeat with other 2 wires. Stick ends of wires deep into chimney.

8. Use a paintbrush to paint craft glue along sides and on top of roof. Generously sprinkle black glitter on glue. Put large glob of hot glue on top of chimney to secure wires and sprinkle with black glitter.

9. Trace bat pattern onto blue construction paper 4 times; cut out. Fold them down the middle, making creases. Dab wings with craft glue; sprinkle lightly with crystal glitter. Use hot glue to secure bats around house.

10. Hot-glue raffia and floral pumpkin around base of house.

Slinky Snake

A slinky snake is a frightful sight, especially when coiled and ready to bite.
But have no fear, my dear, the slinky snake is made of rope, I hear!

WHAT YOU'LL NEED

- Wire cutters
- Wire: 14 gauge, 24 gauge
- Yardstick
- Sandpaper
- 3 feet black braided rope, ⅝-inch diameter
- Paper clay
- Round toothpick
- Acrylic paint: black, yellow
- Paintbrushes: ¼-inch flat, #3

1. Cut a 3-foot, 3-inch piece of 14-gauge wire. Sand one end to a point. Push wire into rope, leaving 1½ inches of wire protruding on each end.

2. At each end, bend ½ inch of wire up. Mold head and tail onto wire with paper clay.

3. Cut two 1-inch pieces of 24-gauge wire. Twist wires together, leaving last ⅛ inch untwisted to form a forked tongue. Insert tongue into front of head. Use toothpick to make nostril holes. Let clay dry.

4. Use ¼-inch brush to paint head, tongue and tail black. Use #3 brush to paint eyes yellow. Let dry.

5. Form body into a coil.

Festive Ware

Scare up an appetite with cookies served on
easy-to-create painted ceramic plates.

WHAT YOU'LL NEED

- Scissors
- Tape
- Glass dinner plate
- Enamel paint for tile, glass or ceramic: dark green, yellow, orange, light green
- Fine-tip paint applicator
- Soft, natural fiber paintbrushes: 1 fine-tip, 1 flat

1. Copy pattern on page 116 several times so pattern will extend around plate, enlarging pattern to fit plate. Cut out patterns and tape around rim with the design facing down. Turn plate upside down.

2. Begin painting by tracing vines with dark green paint and fine-tip applicator.

3. Using fine-tip brush and dark green paint, trace over veins in leaves. With fine-tip applicator and yellow paint, trace over accent lines on pumpkins. Using fine-tip applicator and orange paint, outline pumpkin shapes. Let paint dry 1 hour.

4. With fine-tip applicator and light green paint, trace over leaf outlines and fill in, covering the dark green veins on leaves. With flat brush, fill in pumpkin outlines with orange paint. Apply another coat after 15 to 20 minutes, if needed.

5. Finish by painting pumpkin stem with fine-tip brush and yellow paint. Air dry or bake (according to manufacturer's directions).

Festive Ware, Autumn Leaves (page 58)

Try This! Lure your guests into a web of goodies when they're displayed on this Spiderweb Plate. You'll need many of the same materials you used to create the Pumpkin Vine Plate, plus a disappearing ink pen.

To decorate the plate, turn the plate bottom side up. Using the disappearing ink pen, draw a horizontal line across the center of the plate. Add a vertical line down the center.

Attach an applicator tip to a bottle of black enamel paint. Paint over the horizontal and vertical lines. Add lines with the paint, dividing each quarter until you have the desired number of spokes (8 to 16). Now use paint to create webbing between each of the spokes. Work with 1 spoke at a time, turning the plate as you go.

Let dry for 1 hour before adding spider. Spider is created with the same applicator tip; draw an oval and fill in with paint. Add legs. Let dry or bake (according to manufacturer's directions).

TIP: Occasionally wipe off applicator tip with damp paper towel to keep your lines clean. Use a toothpick to clean up any excess paint. If you are unhappy with your design, wash the plate before the paint dries (within 24 hours).

Boo! Pots

Looking for a quick-and-easy project that is sure to be an eye-catcher?
Then here's Boo! to you with beads and pots.

WHAT YOU'LL NEED

- Serrated knife
- 4×4×2-inch foam block
- 4 clay pots, 3 inches each
- Natural excelsior moss
- Ribbon: 36 inches green, $^3/_4$ inch wide;
    36 inches purple wire-edge, 1$^1/_2$ inches wide
- Pencil
- Scissors
- 2 sheets double-sided super-sticky tape,
    9×6 inches each
- Aluminum armature wire, $^1/_{16}$ inch diameter
- Wire cutters
- Hammer
- Glass or metal baking dish
- Assorted wiggle eyes, 3mm to 28mm
- Tiny glass marbles: purple, green
- Tiny green glass bead mix
- 18-gauge black craft wire
- Round-nose jewelry pliers
- Black "E" beads

1. Use serrated knife to cut foam block into 4 equal blocks. Insert a block into each clay pot, wedging it tightly inside. Remove foam; trim so foam is $^1/_2$ inch below top edge of pot. Replace foam in all pots.

2. Cover foam with excelsior moss. Tuck edges of moss around foam, covering foam completely. Cut both ribbons in half. Wrap top edge of 2 pots with green ribbon, tie a knot and V-cut ribbon ends. Repeat for remaining 2 pots using purple ribbon. Set pots aside.

3. Enlarge and trace 4 O's, 1 backward B, 1 forward B, 2 exclamation points and 2 dots from pattern on page 120 onto super-sticky tape. (Flip pattern to make back of B), Cut out.

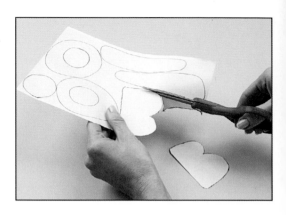

4. Shape aluminum wire into framework for letters and exclamation point, making framework ¼ inch smaller than shapes. Leave a 3½-inch tail at bottom of all shapes. Hammer wire flat.

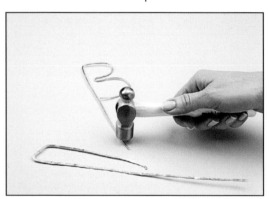

5. Place a B, a backward B and an exclamation point with dot in baking dish. Peel off top protective layer. Press wiggle eyes in place. Pour purple glass marbles over tape to coat. Carefully press marbles into front surface of B and exclamation point to fill any areas that weren't completely coated. Repeat process for all shapes.

Note: For 2 O's (1 front and 1 back), use green glass bead mix, then fill in empty spaces with green glass marbles.

6. Use front of shapes for this step. Remove protective layer from back of bead-coated shape. Place bead-side down onto a flat surface. Press wire framework onto sticky side. Replace protective layer. Attach framework to all letter fronts.

Boo! Pots

7. For backs of all letters, remove backing from unbeaded side. Take off protective layer from letter fronts; apply matching back to each shape. Should edges not match exactly, press appropriate color beads or marbles to coat. Repeat for all shapes. Insert wire tail into each clay pot.

8. Use jewelry pliers to bend and shape black craft wire, creating spooky shapes. Thread "E" beads onto wires and space them throughout shapes. Cut wire ends; insert into clay pots.

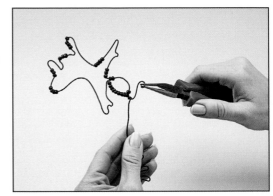

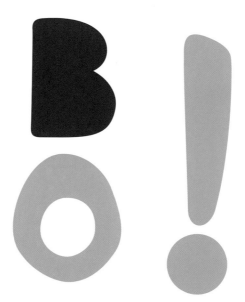

Enlarge Patterns 195%

Spooky Supperware

Add some cackles to your next Halloween meal—it'll be a real nail-biter!
Guests will howl over this spooky set of ghoulishly fun utensils!

WHAT YOU'LL NEED

- Green or white polymer clay
  (2-ounce pack per 2 utensils)
- Oven-safe eating utensils
- Aluminum foil
- Baking pan
- Optional: Red nail polish

1. Preheat oven to 275°F. Condition clay until it is soft and pliable. Roll 1 ounce of clay into log as long as utensil handle. Press handle front firmly into log; work clay around back of handle until handle is covered. Shape clay to create bumpy knuckles.

2. Press round edge of a spoon into fingertip end to make fingernail. Use knife to make crease marks in knuckles.

3. Place finished utensils on foil-covered baking pan. Bake clay for 30 minutes according to manufacturer's instructions.

4. Remove from oven; let cool before using. Paint fingernails, if desired. Hand wash utensils.

Fright Lights

Illuminate the night with simple silhouettes enhanced by vellum and candlelight.

WHAT YOU'LL NEED

- White colored pencil
- Lightweight black paper
- Fine-tip scissors, such as embroidery scissors
- Double-sided cellophane tape
- Ruler
- Rotary cutter or scissors
- 5 sheets orange vellum
- 3 heat-proof candleholders, 6 inches each
- 2 heat-proof candleholders, 8 inches each
     (use containers meant specifically for candles)
- Votive candles

1. Enlarge patterns to fit candleholders and trace patterns onto black paper. Cut out shapes with embroidery scissors. Use small pieces of double-sided tape to affix one shape to front of each candleholder.

2. Using ruler and rotary cutter or scissors, trim vellum so it just reaches top edge of candleholder but is no higher than lip of container.

3. Wrap vellum around candleholders and secure at back with double-sided tape. Place candles in holders; carefully light candles.

Trick or Tip: As with any lit candles, do not leave them unattended. Do not use candles that rise over the rim of the containers.

Fright Lights

Spooky Sparkly Door Charm

Halloween gets glitzy with this fun door charm. Glitter, glow-in-the-dark ghosts and pumpkins with pizzazz accent this festive piece.

WHAT YOU'LL NEED

- Pliers
- Tape measure
- 66 inches lightweight armature or garden wire
- Heavy-duty wire clippers
- Polymer clay: 1 ultralight, 2 black, 2 Granny Smith, 2 glow-in-the-dark
- Baking sheet
- Black acrylic paint
- $1/2$-inch flat paintbrush
- Pasta machine
- Waxed paper
- Translucent liquid clay
- Clay blade
- Glitter: black ice, orange surprise, sparkling snow, majestic purple
- $7/8$-inch leaf shape cutter
- Inks: tangerine, Santa Fe red, passion purple
- Needle tool (or toothpick)
- Paper towels

Note: The higher the number of the pasta machine setting, the thinner you should make the sheet when rolling clay out.

1. Preheat oven to 275°F. With pliers, bend a 1-inch loop of armature wire about 4 inches from end. Twist end of wire below loop about $1^{1}/_{2}$-inches. With long end of wire, make a bend about 8 inches down and double wire back to top. At wire fold, form a $3/4$-inch loop; twist 2 wires together above loop for side branch. To form center branch, make a bend about 12 inches down from top and double wire back to top. Form a 1-inch loop at fold; twist 2 wires together. Form third branch like the first. Twist end of wire around center branch; trim excess wire. Form loops at bottom of each branch into diamonds; curve each branch.

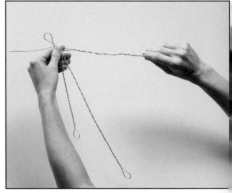

2. Using ultralight clay, pinch off small pieces and cover armature. Bake 20 minutes at 275°F. Let cool; paint top side of clay black. Let dry. Turn piece over; paint back black. Let dry.

Spooky Sparkly Door Charm

3. Pull off a pinch of black clay and set it aside for ghost eyes. Mix remaining black clay with an equal amount of ultralight clay. Roll into several 4×6-inch sheets on #2 setting of pasta machine. Lay a sheet of clay on waxed paper. Spread a thin, even layer of liquid clay over surface. Sprinkle with black ice glitter. Use a swirling motion with fingertip to spread glitter over surface. Add more glitter if necessary. Shake off excess glitter.

Repeat for remaining clay sheets. Use leaf cutter to cut shapes from clay sheets; make about 70 leaves.

4. Place waxed paper on baking tray; lay armature on top. Spread a thin, even coat of liquid clay over branches. Starting at bottom of each branch, attach black leaves in layers until all branches are covered. Add extra liquid clay to attach top layers. Save 8 to 10 leaves for next step. When done placing leaves, bake for 20 to 30 minutes at 275°F. Let cool completely.

5. With Granny Smith clay, roll four 8×$\frac{1}{4}$-inch-thick snakes and two 12×$\frac{1}{4}$-inch-thick snakes. Twist two 8-inch snakes together; taper an end to a point. Squeeze a line of liquid clay down center of a shorter branch; press twisted green stem in place, trimming excess clay at top. Repeat for other branches (12-inch snakes are for center branch). Add remaining leaves over top of stems with liquid clay.

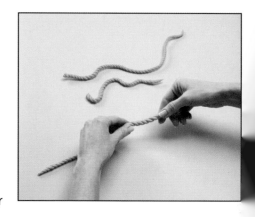

6. Roll a sheet of ultralight clay on #1 setting of pasta machine. Place sheet on waxed paper and squeeze tangerine and Santa Fe red inks over surface of sheet. Let ink dry; knead color into clay. Roll four 1-inch balls. Squeeze a small amount of liquid clay onto a ball. Dip ball into orange surprise glitter. Roll ball between palms to coat it evenly with glitter. Add more liquid clay and glitter if necessary. Tap off excess glitter. Repeat for remaining 3 balls. Gently flatten each ball into an oval and cut ovals in half for pumpkins. Make lines with needle tool. Roll a $\frac{1}{4}$-inch-wide snake of Granny Smith clay and cut eight $\frac{1}{4}$-inch pieces. Add stem texture with needle tool; attach stems to pumpkins with liquid clay.

Roll a long ¹/₁₆-inch-thick snake; cut into 2-inch lengths. Attach 1 to each pumpkin with liquid clay, making a swirl at end. Attach 7 pumpkins to base with liquid clay.

7. Mix glow-in-the-dark clay with an equal amount of ultralight clay. Roll five 1-inch balls from mixed clay.

Flatten a ball into a disk; roll disk through pasta machine on #1 setting and then #2 setting. Turn clay sheet ¼ turn; roll through again on #3 and then #4 setting to make a thin, flat oval of clay. Place sheet on waxed paper and spread a thin, even coat of liquid clay over surface. Sprinkle sparkling snow glitter over surface and swirl with finger for complete coverage. Repeat for remaining 4 ovals. Roll five ⁵/₈-inch balls of mixed clay. Make a ball into a slightly flattened oval. Drape a glittered clay sheet over flattened oval to create ghost. Repeat for other 4 ghosts. Make ten ¹/₁₆-inch balls of black clay. Roll balls into ovals and flatten. Attach 2 ovals to each ghost for eyes. Add liquid clay to back side of each ghost and attach them to base.

8. Roll out a sheet of ultralight clay on #1 setting of pasta machine so piece is about 5×6 inches. Lay clay sheet on waxed paper; cover surface with passion purple ink. Let ink dry completely. Turn sheet over; ink other side. Let dry; mix color into clay. Roll clay into 6-inch-long sheet on #1 setting of pasta machine.

Spread thin coat of liquid clay over surface of sheet. Sprinkle purple glitter over surface; rub it onto sheet using a circular motion. Tap off excess glitter. Flip sheet over; glitter other side. Cut a ⁵/₈-inch-wide strip of clay; cut ends on diagonal. Fold strip into a V for ribbon tails. Put a dot of liquid clay at top of door charm below hanging loop and attach V. Arrange ribbon ends so they flow. Cut 4 strips 6×⁵/₈ inches each. Fold each strip in half, gluing ends together with liquid clay. Attach loops on top of V with liquid clay. Shape bow so it flows. Attach last pumpkin to center of bow with liquid clay.

9. Bake door charm 30 minutes at 275°F; let cool.

Glass Bead Spider

Glittering spiders decorate your house
and surprise your family with their realism.

WHAT YOU'LL NEED

- 26-gauge black wire
- Black round bead
- Teardrop glass bead with black and silver inside
- Black seed beads
- Scissors or wire cutters

1. To make spider body, thread 6 inches of wire through large black bead and teardrop bead. Add a seed bead to end; thread wire back through both beads and add another seed bead. Beads should not be tight against each other. Twist wires at end of spider; insert wire ends into spider body.

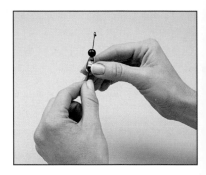

2. Legs are made in pairs. Cut 6 inches of wire; turn up one end. String on 25 seed beads. Fold wire in half, leaving about 1/4-inch space in center unstrung. String 25 seed beads on other half of wire. Bend wire at end and trim. Make additional pair of legs. Make 2 more pairs of legs, threading 30 beads on each side.

3. Twist beaded legs (with longer legs toward back) around spider between large beads of body. Bend legs to make them spiderlike.

Haunted Hint: You can add a spider to your lapel—it's as simple as gluing a jewelry pin to the underside of a finished spider!

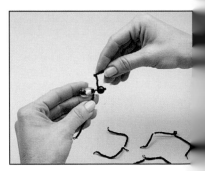

Glass Bead Spiders

Hobnobbing Hobgoblin

This fun creature will set the mood to get your party guests monster-mashing.

WHAT YOU'LL NEED

- Old newspapers
- Black duct tape
- 5 to 6 coat hangers
- Wire cutting pliers
- Flat rocks: two 5-inch long, 3-inches thick
- 10-inch wood dowel or stick
- Scissors
- Measuring tape
- Cardstock
- Paintbrush
- Wood or foam balls, 1$^1/_2$ inches each
- Glow-in-the-dark green acrylic paint
- Craft foam or paper: white, light green
- Permanent marker

1. Wad newspapers into 6-inch ball for head and large egg-shaped body. Completely wrap and cover shapes with duct tape.

2. Using pliers, form two arms with two fingers from coat hangers. Fold a hanger in half, leaving about 3 inches between wires at widest point; place flat rock at widest section. Fold a hanger in half for each leg; place a rock at each end for feet. Wrap all pieces with tape to cover. Fold another hanger in half for neck, taping wood dowel to wire.

3. Use scissors to poke holes to place arms, legs, neck and tail into head and body shapes. Attach wire limbs and neck to body and head pieces with tape.

4. Cut three 6×6×4-inch triangles from cardstock. Cover two triangles with tape for ears. Roll third triangle into tight cone to form long pointy nose; cover nose with tape.

Hobnobbing Hobgoblins

5. Paint wood balls green; let dry. Tape balls to head for eyes; don't cover all of balls with tape. Cut two 2-inch ovals from white foam or paper and cut mouth pieces from light green paper; make pupils in eyes with marker. Position and glue to face. Position and attach wrapped nose and ear pieces with tape.

TIP: This Make other monsters using the same technique. Use different colors of duct tape and your active imagination to create the most fantastical creatures ever! Or craft tried-and-true monsters by decorating recycled items such as boxes, tubes and ice-cream cartons. Glue the pieces together—and have Frankenstein at your command!

Handy Halloween Centerpiece

This centerpiece is hands-on fun for the entire ghostly crew!

WHAT YOU'LL NEED

- Black acrylic paint
- Paintbrush
- 6-inch papier-mâché box
- 63-inch wood rectangle
- Flat craft wood stick
- Hot glue gun, glue sticks
- Anchor pin
- Serrated knife
- Foam block
- Spanish moss
- 10 fern pins
- Fake hand
- Dowel rod, ¼ diameter, cut 8 inches long
- Heavy-duty scissors
- Orange branches
- Rose stem
- Wired curly willow branches
- Brown astilbe stem
- Scrapbook Halloween cutout

1. Paint box, wood rectangle and flat stick black. Let dry. Apply second coat if needed for complete coverage.

2. Glue anchor pin to bottom of box. Cut foam block to fit inside box; place foam on anchor pin. Cover foam with Spanish moss and secure with fern pins.

3. Cut foam to fit inside opening of hand; be sure foam fits snugly to hold shape. Place foam inside hand opening.

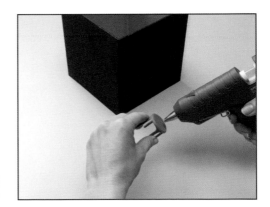

4. Push dowel rod into foam inside hand, pushing dowel to top of hand. Glue exposed portion of dowel into foam in box.

5. Cut orange branches to varying lengths. Glue branches throughout arrangement and glue directly into foam. Cut rose stem to varying lengths; glue throughout.

6. Cut curly willow branches to varying lengths. Glue willow throughout arrangement. Pull astilbe from stem. Glue astilbe throughout.

7. To make sign, glue flat wood stick to rectangle, making rectangle wider than it is long when attached to stick. Glue scrapbook Halloween cutout to wood stick. Glue sign into foam.

It's Halloween!

Handy Halloween Centerpiece

Ghoulish Greeter

Sweep fall into your home with this uniquely scary door hanging.

WHAT YOU'LL NEED

- 26-gauge green wire
- Plastic ghoul face
- Grapevine broom
- 2 orange berry branches
- Measuring tape
- Hot glue gun, glue sticks
- Heavy-duty scissors
- 5 purple ranunculus stems
- Fall leaf stem
- 46 inches double-faced black satin ribbon

1. Wire face to broom. Cut berry branches into 4 sections of varying lengths, between 6 and 10 inches each. Glue branches to grapevine.

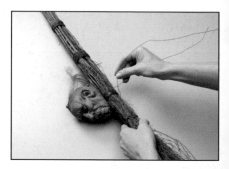

2. Cut ranunculus stems to varying lengths, between 3 and 8 inches each. Glue ranunculus stems to grapevine.

3. Pull individual leaves off stem; glue leaves throughout arrangement. Tuck leaf ends under flowers and berries.

4. Cut four 8-inch pieces of ribbon. From each piece, create a loop by gluing ends together. Glue ribbon loops behind face. Cut two 7-inch-long ribbons; cut ends on an angle. Glue ribbons to arrangement below bow.

Goulish Greeter

Howlin' Hot Pads

Let felt add color to your Halloween kitchen!
These are just the things to hold your warm dinner on cool fall nights.

WHAT YOU'LL NEED

- Pencil
- Double-side fusible iron-on webbing
- Scissors
- Steam iron
- Ironing board
- Felt, 2 squares each: olive, cranberry, white, lavender, purple, kelly green, yellow, orange
- Measuring tape
- Quilt batting
- 3 squares black cotton broadcloth, 11×11 inches each
- Sewing needle
- White thread
- Embroidery floss: sage green, metallic silver, black, tangerine
- Embroidery needle
- 2 metal buttons, $^7/_8$ inch each
- Assorted small and medium buttons
- 2 black "E" beads

1. Enlarge and trace patterns on page 141 onto fusible webbing and cut out. Following manufacturer's directions, iron fusible webbing pieces to back of appropriate color felt. Cut out pieces.

2. For ghost side borders, cut a $^3/_8$×10-inch strip and four 1$^1/_2$-inch squares of fusible webbing. Iron 10-inch strip to olive felt and 1$^1/_2$-inch squares to various felt colors. Cut out.

3. **Candy corn:** Cut four $^3/_4$×10-inch strips fusible webbing. Iron 2 to cranberry felt and 2 to olive. Cut out.

4. For front and back pieces, cut a 9$^1/_4$-inch square from each color felt: lavender, purple, cranberry, olive, kelly green and yellow. From each color felt noted above, cut a $^5/_8$×5$^1/_2$-inch strip for hangers.

5. Refer to photos to place all pieces on felt. Fuse in place. Trim olive and cranberry felt strips on ghost and candy corn pads.

6. Cut three 10-inch squares of quilt batting. Center a batting square on a broadcloth square; place a decorated felt piece on top. Use needle and thread to baste pieces together.

Howlin' Hot Pads, Foot of Meat (page 26)

7. Unless otherwise indicated, work with 3 strands of floss for embroidery. Whipstitch thread ends to secure stitching; go through all layers.

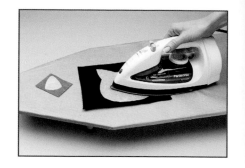

Cat: Using sage green floss, blanket stitch around head and whipstitch around nose. Make mouth as shown on pattern. Use metallic silver floss to stitch metal button eyes in place. Use straight stitches to create eyebrows and a split stitch to make whiskers. Add French knots on nose with silver.

Ghost: Using silver floss, blanket stitch around ghost and sew a running stitch around outer edge of small squares. Using sage green floss, sew a running stitch along side edges of olive felt strip and ¹/₂-inch in from outer edges of large square.

Candy Corn: Using silver floss, make herringbone stitch over yellow and orange and orange and white candy corn edges. Blanket stitch around outer edges of candy corn.

8. Cut three 9-inch squares of quilt batting; center on back of broadcloth. Place a 9¹/₄-inch felt square on back of batting. Place dark purple on back of cat, olive green on back of ghost and yellow on back of candy corn. Baste pieces of each pad together. Trim broadcloth to ¹/₈ inch from outer edges.

9. Stitch through all layers, using 3 strands of floss for embroidery.

Cat: Using black floss, make quilting knots around cat. Trim ends. Using silver floss, do a running stitch around triangles. Stitch button at center of each triangle, knotting 2 and stitching 2.

Ghost: Using black floss, make quilting knots around ghost and sew on "E" beads for eyes. Stitch a button at center of each small square.

Candy Corn: Using sage green floss, do a running stitch at edges of olive strips. Using black floss, do a running stitch on cranberry strips. Stitch a button at each intersection of olive and cranberry strips.

10. Trim all edges even. Blanket stitch edges using 6 strands of floss. Use black for cat and ghost and tangerine for candy corn. Place kelly green and yellow hanger pieces together; blanket stitch edges with tangerine floss.

Place dark purple and lavender pieces together and cranberry and olive pieces together. Blanket stitch each with black floss. Stitch hangers to each pad, matching colors. Stitch a button on top of ends. Remove all basting stitches.

Care Instructions: Hand wash hot pads in cold water; air-dry flat. Gently press if needed.

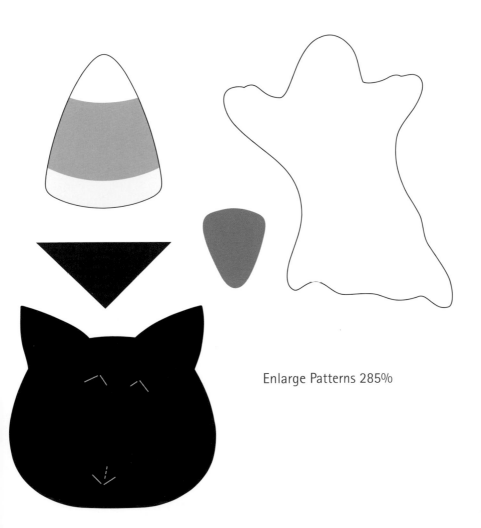

Enlarge Patterns 285%

Acknowledgments

The publisher would like to thank the companies and associations listed below for the use of their recipes in this publication.

The Hershey Company

Kraft Foods Global, Inc.

National Chicken Council / US Poultry & Egg Association

Nestlé USA

VOLUME MEASUREMENTS (dry)

$1/8$ teaspoon = 0.5 mL
$1/4$ teaspoon = 1 mL
$1/2$ teaspoon = 2 mL
$3/4$ teaspoon = 4 mL
1 teaspoon = 5 mL
1 tablespoon = 15 mL
2 tablespoons = 30 mL
$1/4$ cup = 60 mL
$1/3$ cup = 75 mL
$1/2$ cup = 125 mL
$2/3$ cup = 150 mL
$3/4$ cup = 175 mL
1 cup = 250 mL
2 cups = 1 pint = 500 mL
3 cups = 750 mL
4 cups = 1 quart = 1 L

VOLUME MEASUREMENTS (fluid)

1 fluid ounce (2 tablespoons) = 30 mL
4 fluid ounces ($1/2$ cup) = 125 mL
8 fluid ounces (1 cup) = 250 mL
12 fluid ounces ($1 1/2$ cups) = 375 mL
16 fluid ounces (2 cups) = 500 mL

WEIGHTS (mass)

$1/2$ ounce = 15 g
1 ounce = 30 g
3 ounces = 90 g
4 ounces = 120 g
8 ounces = 225 g
10 ounces = 285 g
12 ounces = 360 g
16 ounces = 1 pound = 450 g

DIMENSIONS

$1/16$ inch = 2 mm
$1/8$ inch = 3 mm
$1/4$ inch = 6 mm
$1/2$ inch = 1.5 cm
$3/4$ inch = 2 cm
1 inch = 2.5 cm

OVEN TEMPERATURES

250°F = 120°C
275°F = 140°C
300°F = 150°C
325°F = 160°C
350°F = 180°C
375°F = 190°C
400°F = 200°C
425°F = 220°C
450°F = 230°C

BAKING PAN SIZES

Utensil	Size in Inches/Quarts	Metric Volume	Size in Centimeters
Baking or Cake Pan (square or rectangular)	8×8×2	2 L	20×20×5
	9×9×2	2.5 L	23×23×5
	12×8×2	3 L	30×20×5
	13×9×2	3.5 L	33×23×5
Loaf Pan	8×4×3	1.5 L	20×10×7
	9×5×3	2 L	23×13×7
Round Layer Cake Pan	8×1½	1.2 L	20×4
	9×1½	1.5 L	23×4
Pie Plate	8×1¼	750 mL	20×3
	9×1¼	1 L	23×3
Baking Dish or Casserole	1 quart	1 L	—
	1½ quart	1.5 L	—
	2 quart	2 L	—